Developing Sustainable Supply Chains to Drive Value, Volume II

Developing Sustainable Supply Chains to Drive Value, Volume II

Management Issues, Insights, Concepts, and Tools—Implementation

Robert P. Sroufe
Steven A. Melnyk

BUSINESS EXPERT PRESS

First published in 2017 by
Business Expert Press, LLC
222 East 46th Street, New York, NY 10017
www.businessexpertpress.com

ISBN-13: 978-1-63157-851-9 (paperback)
ISBN-13: 978-1-63157-852-6 (e-book)

Business Expert Press Environmental and Social Sustainability for Business Advantage Collection

Collection ISSN: 2327-333X (print)
Collection ISSN: 2327-3348 (electronic)

Cover and interior design by S4Carlisle Publishing Services Private Ltd., Chennai, India

First edition: 2017

10 9 8 7 6 5 4 3 2 1

Printed in the United States of America.

Abstract

As we enter the 21st century, we find ourselves faced with two major developments. The first is the emergence of the supply chain as a strategic and tactical weapon. With the emergence of the supply chain, the unit of competition has shifted from the firm to the supply chain. However, with the advent of the supply chain, it is important to recognize that we have to view strategic objectives within a context that stresses not simply the internal operations of the firm but also the elements and stakeholders of the supply chain—elements that include the supplier base, customers, logistics linkages, relationships, transparency, and visibility. We realize that the supply chain is no stronger than its weakest link.

The second development is that of sustainability. This paradigm shift is more than simply being environmentally responsible. Rather, it is overall sustainability as measured in terms of the firm's ability to reduce waste, improve profitability, generate strategic competitive advantages, recognize emerging social issues while ensuring that it is safe and treats its employees well. In the past, sustainability was viewed as a marketing fad; this is no longer the case. Sustainability is increasingly becoming at a minimum an expectation and a requirement for doing business (i.e., an order qualifier) and under many conditions something that differentiates firms and makes them more attractive to potential customers (i.e., an order winner).

These two developments, while often treated as separate entities, are very interrelated. It is this interrelationship that forms the major focus and thrust of this book. Essentially what *Developing Sustainable Supply Chains to Drive Value* does is to present the reader with an integrated, business-oriented treatment of sustainable supply chain management (SSCM) that explores why it is no longer enough for a firm to focus on sustainability within only the four walls of the firm. Rather, in today's business environment, sustainability must involve the supply chain in a deliberate and integrated fashion. To succeed with sustainability, a firm must ensure that this outcome is not only present within the firm but is also present within the supply chain. As the insights, tools, and concepts within this book will illustrate, the market and consumers will punish those firms that promise sustainability but that are not able to deliver on this promise because of problems in the supply chain.

Both Volume 1 (Foundations) and Volume 2 (Implementation) are intended to be a stand-alone read for executive education, and supplementary text for existing MBA supply chain management courses. In Volume 2 we start with design for sustainability and design thinking, next we review supporting frameworks and tools before looking at the integration of sustainability and supply chain management, and how to enable people and customers. We then look at sustainable systems as the order winners of the future, review case studies of implementation, and then review successfully implementing sustainable supply chains to drive value before concluding with how emerging supply chain leaders will need a strategic focus with a call for action while recognizing this is just the end of the beginning.

The two-volume set provides an evidence-based management approach to sustainability and value chains to allow understanding from a variety of disciplines and professional backgrounds. If you are a business professional wanting a 2- to 3-hour introduction to SSCM, we suggest you review Volume 1 so you can more quickly be ready to put learning into action, whether at the office or in the classroom. For a more in-depth understanding of SSCM as a driver of value, we can't help but recommend you read each volumes, while fully engaging in the action-learning process.

Key features of this two-volume set include, but are not limited to:

- Short vignettes of important trends to start each chapter.
- Relevant management issues.
- Evidence-based management examples from leading multinational companies along with small and medium enterprises spanning supply chains.
- References to appropriate tools, emerging technology, and practices.
- Interdisciplinary perspectives enabling your own ability to implement and manage a more sustainable supply chain.
- Chapter Action Items and Audit Questions for the reader to take a deeper look at integration opportunities involved in sustainability and supply chain management.
- An action-learning approach to applying concepts and tools.
- Guidelines on how to move forward with a supply chain sustainability initiative.

Keywords

action learning, audits, benefits, best in class, business models, carbon, carbon disclosure project (CDP), carbon footprint, circular economy, collaboration, culture, design for sustainability, dashboard, design thinking, enablers, energy management, environmental profit & loss statement, environmental management systems, environmental protection agency, environmental standards, framework for strategic sustainable development (FSSD), freight, greenhouse gas (GHG) protocol, global reporting initiative (GRI), greenhouse gas emissions, implementation, innovation, integration, integrated bottom line, less than truckload, life cycle assessment, metrics, multicriterion decision analysis, natural capital, new product development, obstacles, operationalize, order losers, order winners, performance measurement, pollution prevention, process design, product design, quality management, self-audit, social capital, social sustainability, supplier assessment, supply chain operations reference model, smart way program, supply chain management, sustainability, system design, systems thinking, standards, sustainability portfolio, sustainable value added (SVA), the natural step, toolkit, tools, total quality management, transparency, triple bottom line, trends, United Nation's Sustainable Development Goals (SDGs), universal breakthrough sequence, value generation, waste.

Contents

Acknowledgments

We would like to thank the many people and organizations that contributed their support to this book. We need to thank MBA Sustainability Fellows Derek McMahan, Laura Monahan, Gina Johnson, Claudia Osorno, and Velika Talyarkhan for their research assistance and refinement of the chapters. Next, we would like to thank Duquesne University and the Alcoa Foundation for funding the fellowship program and portions of the research within this book; the Beard Institute for their continued support of interdisciplinary projects involving sustainability; and Michigan State University. We would not be able to include compelling information about companies already pushing the sustainability performance frontier if it were not for the many local and national companies and organizations that provided insight and examples for this book. Therefore, we need to thank 3M, Applied Products, Alcoa, Baxter, Bayer Material Sciences, Dow, DuPont, EMC, FedEx, Ford, GaBi, Global Reporting Initiative, General Motors, Herman Miller, H.J. Heinz, Honeywell, IBM, Johnson & Johnson, Office Depot, Proctor & Gamble, Pitt Ohio, UPMC, Wesco, and Westinghouse. And finally, we would like to thank our families for supporting us and enabling the development of this book. To our children, we hope you will someday live in a sustainable world. To the readers of this book, we hope that you will spearhead the changes that make it possible for our children and all future generations to live in a sustainable world.

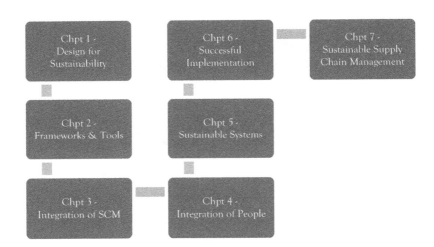

The Key Activities of a Sustainable Supply Chain

CHAPTER 1

Design for Sustainability— Collectively Transforming Systems and Process

Design is the first signal of human intention.
—Bill McDonough, in the documentary,
The Next Industrial Revolution

Where can you find evidence of substantial change and the impacts of sustainability on products, processes, and supply chains? Design and the use of environmental AND social metrics have together culminated in new insight, cost savings, impact reduction, and differentiation as a result of leveraging sustainability for operations and supply chains. Examples include:

- MillerCoors has recognized that its products (beer) have a major impact on society. Consequently, it has developed and implemented a comprehensive program that embraces all aspects of sustainability— the social, environmental, and financial capital. This is a plan that is moving MillerCoors toward reducing the amount of water needed to make one gallon of beer—the goal is 3:1 in an industry where craft breweries typically use anywhere from 6 to 10 gallons to make one gallon of beer. The plan involves developing a sustainable supply chain through collaboration and education. The plan also involves MillerCoors helping communities deal with the adverse effects of drinking by focusing on reducing/eliminating underage drinking and on encouraging responsible consumption and designated drivers. Through the plan, MillerCoors has set a goal to ensure that by 2020

43 percent of the management will consist of women and minorities. It is a plan that strives to change the culture of MillerCoors. The results have positively affected MillerCoors' public image, its top line (revenue) and its bottom line (profits).

- Amazon, one of the world's largest e-retailers, has embraced sustainability both within the company and in the supply chain. It has focused on improving the sustainability of packaging within the supply chain, beginning with the packaging at Amazon. Consequently, it has introduced Frustration-Free Packaging—programs designed to promote shipping products in their own packages without additional shipping boxes and easy-to-open, 100 percent recyclable packaging. These initiatives have grown to include over 1.2 million products and have eliminated more than 36,000 tons of excess packaging in 2015 alone. Amazon has also pushed sustainability through the supply chain by requiring each supplier to ensure that their suppliers and subcontractors conform to the standards and practices of Amazon's Supplier Code of Conduct—a standard that covers areas such as health and safety in production and working areas, the right to legal wages and benefits, prevention of child labor or forced labor, and fair and ethical treatment (including nondiscrimination). Amazon has been known to terminate any supplier that either violates the Code or does not cooperate with the auditors.

- McKinsey and Co predicts $380 billion in potential annual net material cost-saving opportunities in the European Union (EU) from the adoption of "circular" business practices. In this system, value is created by looping products, components, and materials back into the value chain after they fulfill their utility over the life of the product. To realize the full resource productivity opportunity, firms will need to work across circular supply chains, analyze how raw materials are extracted, components produced, products designed, and how return markets are organized, while also considering new business models such as leasing products to customers to retain ownership of materials embedded in the products.[1]

---

[1] McKinsey and Co. (2012).

These examples illustrate the new opportunities available from a better understanding of products, processes, and supply chains. In this chapter, we discuss the evolution of design trends, stress the importance of educating management as to the importance of design thinking, and the utilization of well-known stage-gate product design processes. We review our own research regarding the adoption of sustainability practices by different categories of firms (Innovators, Early Adopters, Early Majority, Late Majority, and Laggards), followed by a discussion of what it will take to cross the sustainability chasm to integrate better design into current practices. To help operationalize this integration, we review important new opportunities to design with less energy and materials, planning, and project assessment.

Objectives

1. Understand what firms are doing to integrate sustainability into stage-gate new product design processes.
2. See opportunities through a design and systems thinking lens.
3. Leverage Design for Sustainability (DfS) to improve product and process efficiency.

Introduction

The product or service design decisions organizations make are linked to sustainability and strategy. It's hard to know why Apple made the decision to stop certification of its products by Electronic Product Environmental Assessment Tool (EPEAT), a green computing standard.[2] This important standard moved the product-labeling sector toward more detailed product assessment and was supported by an Executive Order in 2007, requiring all U.S. government agencies to procure 95 percent EPEAT-registered products. As a result of Apple's actions and the decision to stop utilizing this product standard, whole cities such as San Francisco have blocked Mac purchases.

---

[2] Green Research (2012).

The reality for Apple and other electronics manufacturers is that there is no single definition of a "green product." The manufacture, use, and disposal of IT products can have a wide range of environmental impacts. Some products may have excellent environmental performance in some dimensions, such as energy efficiency or the absence of toxic materials, but substandard performance in other dimensions, such as raw material extraction and transportation. Apple has performed life cycle assessments (LCAs) of its products and found that 91 percent of the greenhouse gas (GHG) emissions associated with its products are traceable to the manufacturing and use phase. It traced just 2 percent of its GHG emissions to recycling. Some issues have come up with glued-together components of products such as the MacBook Pro. Armed with more detailed LCA information, Apple has the opportunity to revisit product design and marketing options regarding product labeling. While this product offering is lighter, and has more power, customers cannot take it apart, and it cannot be upgraded or recycled. These product attributes result in order losses for many who have been happy with Mac offerings in the past.

Apple has a history of sending mixed messages when it comes to sustainability and customer engagement. At the time of writing this book, Apple's newest laptop, the MacBook Pro with Retina display, has taken a substantially unimpressive reversal in recyclability, which means the product did not qualify for EPEAT certification. When the news broke, Apple reacted by pulling ALL its computers from the EPEAT program and claiming that customers valued design over sustainability. Customers, including the city of San Francisco, were quick to disagree, and just as quickly as they had reacted, Apple had not only returned to the EPEAT standard but assigned the latest (still not recyclable) laptop an EPEAT gold rating. This mixed messaging and struggles with standards and customer expectations highlights the importance of strategic alignment of sustainability. Apple's strategy could use a closer look at business model alignment, the closed-loop capabilities of its products and processes, and key customer engagement. Apple already designs very attractive products, and they appear to have strayed from earlier "green" product attributes and again need to design sustainability into their products and processes.

When looking for your own opportunities for integrating sustainability, look at any problem from a different perspective than your function.

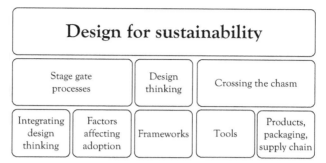

Figure 1.1 The design architecture

Start with an understanding of strategy and ask questions regarding how environmental and social performance can be included in design processes. This can be a new way of thinking. A design-thinking approach to any product or process refers to the methods and processes for investigating ill-defined problems, acquiring information, analyzing, and positing solutions early in the design and planning process.

Within this chapter, we want readers to take a step back from their own processes and look at the world as designers. With this in mind, we first look at the origins of DfS and well-known stage-gate processes for integrating sustainability metrics and decision criteria into decision-making practices. DfS has been applied to developing economies, city planning, architecture and is defined as "requiring awareness of the full short and long-term consequences of any transformation of the environment. Sustainable design is the conception and realization of environmentally sensitive and responsible expression as a part of the evolving matrix of nature."[3]

We will review the chapter design topics (Figure 1.1) while presenting evidence of the growth of DfS, we identify trends that will remain important to operations and supply chain managers, and highlight how firms across industries are crossing a chasm into new territory. By the end of the chapter, we review frameworks and tools available to help enable operations and supply chain professionals to identify sustainability opportunities. Finally, we take a look at metrics before reviewing a step-by-step approach to design practices.

---

[3] McDonough and Partners (1992).

As seen in the concepts of just-in-time (JIT)/Lean, total quality management (TQM), and time-based competition (TBC), waste is any activity or product that consumes resources or creates costs without generating any form of offsetting value stream. GHGs are yet another form of waste. We know that managers can minimize waste by changing the way new products are designed. Those firms who include environmental and social issues in the design process have the opportunity to engage customers, utilize new data, reduce disposal costs and permit requirements, avoid environmental fines, better utilize raw materials, boost profits, discover new business opportunities, rejuvenate employee morale, and improve the state of the environment.

Ideally, the most appropriate place for considering sustainability issues is in the design phase since the amount of waste generated is a direct consequence of decisions made during product and process design. DfS is a component of manufacturing and supply chain management and involves making environmental and social considerations an integral part in the design of a product. The concept originated from industry's effort to target specific "environmental" objectives for design engineers to incorporate when creating a new product. DfS has evolved to integrate environmental and social considerations into the design and redesign of products, processes, and management systems. The goals of sustainability can more easily be achieved when environmental issues are identified and resolved during early stages of product and process design, when changes can be made to reduce or eliminate environmental waste.[4]

Most of the research aimed at the development and evaluation of new environmental tools, and procedures focuses on the design stage. This emphasis recognizes the importance of DfS to the overall success of waste reduction and elimination. We now realize that product design, while actually responsible for a relatively small percentage (approx. 5 to 10 percent) of the total costs, has a significant impact on the actual costs incurred within the system. Some estimate that up to 85 percent of life cycle costs are committed by the end of the preliminary design stages. For thirty years now, we have known that at least 50 percent of the costs for a

---

[4] Allenby (1993).

class of mature products are design determined and that up to 70 percent of costs are determined by manufacturing process decisions.

When viewed in this light, it is expected that more managers will be interested in the implementation and use of DfS procedures and tools. Managers will also want to look at DfS issues during the redesign or reengineering of a product or process. Redesign and reengineering typically occur during the maturity or decline phase of the product life cycle, however the time in which a firm is rethinking a product or process is not the only opportunity for DfS practices. After all, DfS involves the identification and elimination of in-process waste streams before they actually occur. However, for most firms, DfS has not achieved the same degree of acceptance as have JIT/Lean, TQM, and TBC. Our research in this area has shown that the level of acceptance of sustainability practices and principles remains very uneven. Some firms such as 3M, Bayer, Baxter, Dow Chemical, DuPont, Herman Miller, Intel, Interfaces, L'Oreal, P&G, Puma, and Timberland, to name a few, have tried to incorporate these concerns into the design process and evaluate product performance not only in terms of costs and profit but also in terms of environmental outcomes. For other firms, DfS remains a perceived constraint—as something that adversely affects the ability of the firm to deliver better products to the marketplace.

Product designers need to understand sustainability opportunities and be able to influence process design. Instead, top management's focus is on regulatory constraints, the slow corporate decision-making process, and cost. Engineering-based design evaluations have long been cited as obstructing environmental and social issues from being an integral part of product design.[5] As you will see, DfS changes are already happening.

Product Design and DfS

The product design process is one of the major tasks for any firm, responsible for two major types of design activities: (a) new product design and development, (b) process design and development. Both product and process designs are closely interrelated and greatly influence each other while

---

[5] Bhat (1993).

Figure 1.2 Cooper's stage-gate new product development model

simultaneously impacting the environment. Both aspects must be considered to ensure that the firm has developed and implemented effective and efficient designs and processes. These design activities (Figure 1.2), in general, present opportunities for firms to find solutions to environmental issues and social issues. When combined, the two design activities shape the scope of the transformation process by determining the types of inputs required and outputs created. Inputs involve substitution of less hazardous alternatives for previously hazardous materials. Some outputs are desirable (e.g., cars built) while others, such as pollution and waste (i.e., GHG emissions), are not.

The product development process embodies all of the steps necessary to take the product from concept to full production. Recently, this process has undergone extensive revision and rethinking due to increased market pressures to reduce the total cycle lead time (from concept to full production), reduce cost, enhance product flexibility, improve product quality, and leverage new tools such as LCA and information. These pressures are some of the same forces that impact prior developments such as TQM, JIT/Lean, TBC, and mass customization.

To reduce total cycle lead time, managers have turned to the development of processes characterized by the use of multifunctional teams and close interaction of the team members over the period of the initial design. This multifunctional teaming and interaction is also integrative in terms of the breadth of the manufacturing system. Examples can be seen in the consideration of not only issues of design but also issues pertaining to manufacturing planning and execution. This reorganization of the design and delivery process has been referred to by such names as simultaneous engineering and concurrent engineering.

One can envision the process (i.e., product/process design and delivery system) as consisting of linked stages: discovery and idea generation; scoping; building the business case; development; testing and validation; launch; and finally postlaunch review.[6] Between each stage is a decision-making gate. The go/no-go gates provide an organized approach to assessment of easier-to-manage innovation and new product design processes. In all stages of the new product development (NPD) process, environmental and sustainability factors must be considered in addition to all other objectives and issues. Furthermore, one function or group no longer manages each activity in isolation. Rather, there is integration of multiple groups or stakeholders, both internally, with other functions, and externally with stakeholders, customers, and suppliers. In the earlier stages of development process, meeting the needs of stakeholders "such as key customers and regulators" is important. In the later stages of this stage-gate process, working with special interest groups and third-party endorsement of products becomes important. The stage-gate model processes include the following:

> *The discovery stage* contains prework designed to discover opportunities and to generate new ideas. The current focus is on innovation and design thinking, understanding the needs of key customers while leveraging technology, transportation, and closed-loop supply chains. Scoping is a preliminary analysis of each project. It provides inexpensive information through basic research to enable narrowing the number of projects. This stage can be a first screen for environmental AND social attributes using known standards (reporting using the global reporting initiative [GRI], ISO 14001, ISO 26000, SA8000) and simple checksheet approaches to identifying potential attributes.

---

[6] Cooper (1993).

Building the business case is a more detailed analysis by primary marketing and technical research. The business case must include the product definition, justification, and a project plan. Here are opportunities to identify LCA impacts and alternative materials and processes, financial performance projections and top line growth, sustainable value added (SVA), sustainable performance review of a supply base, and supply chain analysis and optimization considering variables such as GHG emissions, timing and modes of transportation within given markets.

Development is the detailed design and development of the product along with some preliminary product tests. At this time, a production plan and a market launch plan are developed, including exploration of available environmental and sustainable certifications such as C2C, product labeling, Environmental Product Declaration (EPDs), and applicable ISO certifications.

Testing and validation take a deeper dive into product tests in the marketplace, the lab, and the manufacturing process. This deeper look at processes includes supplier auditing of social AND environmental performance and measurement of product/process impacts such as GHG emissions.

Launch is the beginning of full production, marketing, (if possible, eco-labeling) and selling. Market launch, production and operations, distribution, quality assurance, and reverse logistics should include postlaunch reviews and updated information for corporate sustainability reporting aligned with the GRI, materiality assessment, Carbon Disclosure Project (CDP), and information for stakeholder inquiry such as socially responsible investors and fund analysts.

The stage-gate model is generalizable and, with minimal modification, accommodates environmental and social considerations into each gate and screening process. Of course, it will be necessary to drill down into more firm-specific detail of the subactivities to provide insight and operational instructions for any innovation team. Our own work with firms taking this approach simply starts early in the discovery and scoping stages with a screen for environmental and social performance indicators. A simple checksheet goes a long way toward engaging others in how and why financial, AND environmental, AND social performance can be considered early in any product development process.

There are a number of advantages to using the stage-gate model for product development, which typically result from its ability to identify problems and assess progress before the project's conclusion. Poor projects can be quickly flagged and rejected by disciplined use of the model and gated processes. When using the stage-gate model on a large project, the process can help reduce complexity of what could be a large and limiting innovation process into a straightforward rule-based approach. When a stage-gate model incorporates cost and fiscal analysis tools such as net present value (NPV), and economic value added (EVA), management can project quantitative information regarding the feasibility of developing potential product ideas. In the not too distant future, this model will also include SVA. Finally, the stage-gate process includes an opportunity to validate the business case by a project's executive sponsors. Other advantages include but are not limited to:

- Well-organized innovation process as a source of competitive advantage.
- Prevents poor products in early stages and helps to redirect them.
- Recognizes environmental waste and social sustainability opportunities early in process planning.
- Accelerated product development, a necessity of shorter product life cycles.
- Increases success of new products.
- Breaks down complex innovation process within large organizations into smaller pieces.
- Provides overview, prioritization, and focus.
- Integration and market orientation.
- Cross functionality, utilizing input and participation of employees from various functions.
- Can be combined with various performance metrics such as the SVA concept.

One issue with the stage-gate process is the potential for structural organization to interfere with creativity, as overly structured processes may cause creativity to be reduced in importance. Other limitations include:

- This is set up as a sequential approach to innovation, yet some believe innovation should be organic and organized in parallel with feedback loops.
- Tensions exist between organizing and creativity. Both are important to innovation.
- The stage-gate process needs to be modified to include a top-down link to the business strategy if applied to nonproduct development projects.

The end of the product development process creates several important outcomes, such as the design and introduction of the product, the determination of the types and quantities of materials used, and various processing characteristics (i.e., equipment needed, transportation optimization, closed-loop supply chains, and intermodal options). When taken together, the product design process sets in place the material and capacity requirements, establishes the cost and performance traits of the product, and determines the types and timing of waste streams created and when these waste streams will be created.

The design activities are strongly cross-functional in nature. That is, to be successful from both a corporate and marketing perspective, the product design activities must consider the perspectives of multiple parties and stakeholders.[7] Perspectives included come from internal areas such as marketing, product engineering, finance, manufacturing, production and inventory control, accounting, manufacturing engineering, quality assurance, top management, and external stakeholders such as stockholders, suppliers, government, competitors, special interest groups, the environment, and the customer.

The importance of the gates should not be overlooked. The role of the gate is to ensure that all of the major concerns, objectives, and issues present in the preceding stage have been addressed before permitting the process to continue to the next stage. At these gates, different factors affect sustainability initiatives such as formal information systems, the presence of a green corporate culture; and the use of different tools, metrics, and

---

[7] Polonsky et al. (1998).

available options for energy reduction and waste minimization. During decision-making times between stages, management has the opportunity to generate new practices from environmental, social, and sustainability issues that were formerly viewed as obstacles, but now become opportunities for innovative firms looking for competitive advantage.

While gates are critical to the innovation process, they do not provide insight as to the creation of new ideas and what is typically found within Research and Design (R&D) functions. To better understand what the innovation creation process may look like, we next draw from the design thinking paradigm to help focus on one component of the business model, key customers.

Design Thinking: Reinvent Products, Processes, and Supply Chains for Customers

Design thinking is a human-centered approach to innovation that draws from the designer's toolkit to integrate the needs of people, the possibilities of technology, and the requirements for business success.
                    —Tim Brown, President and CEO of IDEO

Design thinking refers to the methods for investigating ill-defined problems, acquiring information, analyzing, and proposing solutions in the planning and design fields. It is generally considered the ability to understand the context of a problem, creativity in the generation of insights, and rationality to fit solutions to the context. In recent years, design thinking has become an increasingly important part of design and engineering practices, as well as business and management. Its broader use in creative thinking and action learning is having an increasing influence on contemporary education across disciplines. The IDEO approach is currently being used by Duquesne University (Pittsburgh, PA) for teaching and applying design activities within its MBA sustainability program. In this respect, it is similar to systems thinking in understanding and solving problems.

The design process is what puts design thinking into action. It's a structured ethnographic approach to generating and improving ideas. Its phased approach helps to navigate the development from identifying a design challenge to finding and developing a solution. It is a human-centered approach that relies on your ability to be intuitive, to interpret what you observe, and to develop ideas that are emotionally meaningful to those customers you are designing for. The design process consists of discovery, interpretation, ideation, experimentation, and evolution. The result of the process should be: innovative products, processes and services found at the confluence of viability, desirability, sustainability, and feasibility. For those utilizing design thinking, this approach translates into new, innovative avenues for growth grounded in business viability and market desirability.

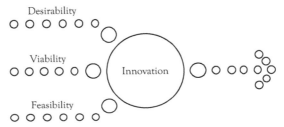

The innovation design process and its major inputs

Currently, there is momentum to expand awareness about design beyond designers and related professions, by teaching design thinking in both industry and higher education. The premise is that by knowing about the process and the methods that designers use to ideate, and by understanding how designers approach problems to try to solve them, individuals, businesses, and business students coming into the workforce will be able to better connect with and invigorate their ideation processes in order to take innovation to a higher level. The goal is to create a competitive advantage in today's global economy and interconnected supply chains.

How Firms Integrate Sustainability and Design: Crossing the Chasm to Design Sustainable Solutions

To better understand the integration of sustainability into design processes, we draw from a modified version of Moore's (1991) Technology Adoption Life Cycle model.[8] This model has five categories of firms:

---

[8] Moore (1991).

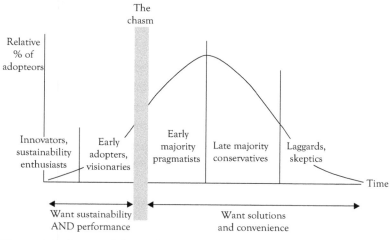

Figure 1.3 Sustainability adoption life cycle

Source: Modified from Sroufe et al. (2000).

Innovators, Early Adopters, Early Majority, Late Majority, and Laggards (see Figure 1.3). We see these same categories of firms in our own research and find generalizable attributes of these firms within their different approaches to sustainability and DfS.

An interesting aspect of Moore's model is the identification of gaps between the categories of firms. These gaps are defined as the amount, or the level of resistance that must be overcome before the group will accept the innovation. With slight modification to fit DfS practices, the gaps signify the difficulties firms and industries may have with sustainability. The largest gap, the "chasm," separates the Early Adopters from the Early Majority. This chasm is important because the acceptance of sustainability initiatives, amount of time, and resources allocated, type of culture necessary, presence of tools or measures available, and sustainability options explored are vastly different on either side. The gaps between the other categories of firms are not as clear, and do not impact the acceptance of sustainability initiatives as strongly as the chasm. The chasm can be described in what the Early Adopter is pursuing as firms to the left of the chasm are perceived *change agents* with a competitive advantage. The chasm is a gap between different levels of sustainability and DfS practices. To understand where your own firm may stand or to help identify other firms within a given industry spectrum, we offer the following attributes of each category of firms.

The *Innovators* pursue new sustainability management techniques aggressively because unique environmental resources are central to their manufacturing process. These firms may have integrated sustainability in the past because it was right for them given the existing cross-functional culture, ability to measure performance on multiple dimensions, and business environment they faced. Sustainability and innovation are considered part of the formal corporate culture. Innovators promote their green culture, market "green" or "eco-labeled" products, and seek new technology for specialized information, pollution prevention, more effective public relations programs, require more frequent auditing, reporting, management reviews and policy improvements. These firms develop an integrated and formal DfS process in order to have a unique resource (e.g., management and decision support systems) and specialized information to aid in decision-making. They find that enhanced financial performance and competitive advantage can come from the design process. There are not many Innovators, but their success is key, because their endorsements reassure other firms that new environmental initiatives do in fact work.

A commonly used example of an Innovator is the General Electric (GE) Company. GE launched Ecomagination based on four commitments: (a) double the investment in R&D for cleaner technologies; (b) increase revenues from Ecomagination products; (c) reduce GHG emissions and improve the energy efficiency of GE's operations; and (d) keep the public informed. These commitments represent ambitious goals for GE and reflect the broader challenges their customers and society face. Drawing on their global capabilities, strengths in technology and knowledge of markets around the world give GE the ability to build a broad portfolio of innovative solutions to a range of energy and environmental challenges. In this context, GE Global Research has formed an Ecoassessment Center of Excellence that provides focused expertise in LCA, end of life and transportation of materials in the environment, and human health/eco risk assessment.

While many factors affect an organizations' adoption of sustainability practices, the drivers tend to be the formal cross-functional responsibility found within these firms, teams within the organization, corporate socially responsible culture, the use of environmental and social performance measures, and the presence of a sustainability functional unit. Motivations for implementing DfS activities are impacted by corporate culture. In some situations, the CEO dictates the corporate social responsibility (CSR) culture; while in others, environmental champions within functional areas will lead the way.

More innovative firms tended to have environmental specialists and engineers (Apple, Interface, Nike, PepsiCo, Stonyfield Farms, Toyota, Unilever) even climate scientists (Ford) involved in all of the design processes and they value the inclusion of sustainability performance measures in individual and corporate performance assessment.

Early Adopters are much like Innovators, having bought into new environmental concepts early in the concept's life cycle, but unlike Innovators, their corporate culture does not emphasize sustainability. Rather, Early Adopters are firms who find it easy to conceptualize or understand the first mover benefits of sustainability initiatives, and relate these potential benefits to their objectives. These firms tend to look at initiatives from an anticipatory performance measurement and cost savings perspective. Early Adopters do not rely on well-established references in making sustainability initiative decisions; they instead prefer to rely on intuition, vision, and developing their own business case for sustainability. Early Adopters become the key to opening up new sustainability initiatives in technology or the adoption of new standards. Adoption of DfS or environmental standards such as EMAS, and ISO 14000 are directly aimed at financial enhancement and competitive advantage. The driving forces for improvements are to seek new technology for waste reduction, pollution prevention, more effective public communication programs, some green labeling of products, auditing and reporting, and frequent management reviews and policy improvements. Early Adopters find the factors affecting value (i.e., flexibility, lead time, cost), the market, and performance measurement to be important to the integration of sustainability issues into new product design. While the design process itself may be formal, there are components of the process that formally and informally integrate sustainability issues. Informal integration is typically the work of a sustainability champion, and formal processes involved checksheets, cross-functional information systems, and a sign-off at each stage or gate of the product development process.

The *Early Majority* shares the Innovator's and Early Adopter's ability to relate to new sustainability initiatives, but is driven by practicality. Our prior research has shown these firms are risk averse, and thereby content to wait and see how others are progressing before they adopt or invest in an initiative. Early Majority firms need a compelling, verifiable reason to change. Sustainability issues are seen as more of an opportunity than an integrated part of business processes. The driving force for sustainability improvements is the threat of current and changing future industry norms, the appearance of potential risk, and regulation. The Early Majority look at sustainability initiatives such as DfS opportunistically and informally. The Early Majority and Late Majority focus more on the elements of value, with budgets sometimes constraining their efforts.

The *Late Majority* consider the costs of new sustainability projects too high to handle. As a result, they wait until there is an established standard before starting a new initiative and showing support. Thus, the importance of established standards discussed in Volume 1, Chapter 4. Late Majority firms see the driving force for environmental improvements as favorable public perception of company operations, avoidance of legal liabilities, and protection of the firm's reputation. Sustainability initiatives are looked at only periodically and informally. The Late Majority tend to consider more carefully the trade-offs concerning the allocation of the budget and resources to environmental projects.

The final classification of the firms is the *Laggard*. These firms are last to adopt sustainability, and simply do not want anything to do with new social or environmental initiatives for a variety of reasons. The only time they will buy into initiatives such as DfS is when it is a critical part of their product or when an external group (e.g., customers or regulators) forces it upon them. The drivers for sustainability improvements are current regulations and industry norms. Laggards are reactive, focusing primarily on governmental regulations (specifically Occupational Safety and Health Act [OSHA], Resource Conservation and Recovery Act [RCRA], Waste Electronic and Electrical Equipment [WEEE], and Regulation Evaluation, Authorization and Restriction of Chemicals [REACH] regulatory requirements) to drive sustainability policy. For Laggards, sustainability, if it is considered, is the job of the Environmental Health and Safety function and lawyers. Typically, an environmental problem (spill, accident, or injury) is what will prompt action from a Laggard, rather than seeking opportunities for CSR and resource efficiency.

Crossing the Chasm

Firms can, and have, crossed the chasm to improve their sustainable business practices. The existence of the chasm does not, in itself, stop the evolution of firms in integrating sustainability business practices. Instead, the chasm represents the greater amount of effort needed by a firm to have a proactive stance on sustainable business practices. Innovators and Early Adopters have formally integrated sustainability issues into the new product design process within firms such as 3M, Bayer, Dow, DuPont, L'Oreal, Herman Miller, Timberland, and Unilever to name a few. Examples can be found within formal processes that integrate environmental concerns within each step of the stage-gate design process. LCA software, databases, and information systems are in place to aid in decision-making. Being the first to adopt, the Innovators and Early Adopters expect to get a jump on the competition via a specialized asset. This jump on the competition can take on several forms, that is, unique resources, reputation, and brand image, legal restrictions to entry and access to new markets, perceived risk reduction by investors, lower product costs, waste reduction, energy reduction, more complete customer service, or other advantages that include employee attrition, learning, and productivity. By contrast, the Early Majority want productivity improvements for existing operations. DfS will be seen as a way to minimize the discontinuity with the old ways of doing business. By the time these firms adopt DfS, they expect it to work properly and to integrate with their existing systems and standards. The Early Majority and other firms to the right of the chasm take a more opportunistic, or periodic, and informal approach to sustainability. These firms may not have formal systems that help with environmental issues during product development. Instead, these firms may rely on individual champions to address environmental problems when they arise. The Laggards may not even consider sustainability issues. It has been suggested by Lubin and Esty that sustainability is a strategic imperative for firms.[9] Within this context, the authors suggest leadership needs to have a vision of sustainability and understanding of the value creation process to start. Next, management needs to establish and integrate execution capabilities of which, we know design is a critical element. Whether your firm is involved in assessment, strategy development, or integration, the use of DfS will shape your thinking, manufacturing, and delivery of goods and services in new and profound ways. Crossing the chasm with a focus on value creation and performance metrics may be what enables your firm to take advantage of the sustainability megatrend.

Leveraging Metrics

As shown in Volume 1, Chapter 3 (which deals with performance measures and metrics), if you do not measure sustainable business practices, you cannot manage sustainable business practices and no one can be held accountable. The idea that metrics and tools are in themselves a solution is a false assumption. Instead, the presence of metrics and tools is an observable *attribute* that helps to verify the presence of sustainability practices and helps a firm to monitor and control its sustainability or DfS practices. The presence or lack of sustainability metrics can be seen in the chasm between the Early Adopters and the Early Majority. The state of performance metrics is a good indicator of the status of sustainability within firms. Innovators have extensive metrics present within their formal system for product development. The metrics can be firm-wide metrics for waste reduction and economic value added, or they can be individually based measures of design speed, cost, and environmental quality. While Early Adopters also have metrics, these firms tend to focus more on the wastes generated from the manufacturing process as a benchmark. Those firms to the right of the chasm lack sustainability measures, and instead rely heavily on environmental regulatory limits of waste generation. These firms tend to think that if they meet the minimum regulatory requirements, everything is fine, yet they miss out on the environmental and economic benefits obtained by leading firms.

---

[9] Lubin and Esty (2010).

A significant difference exists on either side of the chasm when considering the tools available to manage sustainability issues. Innovators and Early Adopters actively use environment management systems (EMS), LCA, and DfS tools. The separation between the Innovators and Early Adopters is found in the amount of familiarity and availability of these tools across functions. Those firms right of the chasm lack decision-making tools for sustainability; they may have some sort of EMS available to aid decision-making, but do not use these systems or reward for this type of job performance.

The focus on options such as EMS, DfS, LCA, and GHG emission metrics, pollution prevention, reduction, reuse, outsourcing, energy conservation, recycling, and water conservation can be found throughout many firms, especially Innovators and Early Adopters. Interestingly, we see a greater need for justification of sustainability projects and return on investment (ROI) coming into play on the right side of the chasm for the Early Majority. In addition, Late Majority firms may try to spread environmental risks to supply chain members. This can be done by outsourcing hazardous processes, or by having someone else process and dispose of the waste generated on site. As would be expected by reactive firms such as the Laggards, sustainability options and opportunities are not even considered.

While much of our focus is on the chasm between the Early Adopters and Early Majority, the effort needed for firms to move from no action (Laggards) to some action (Late Majority) will constitute a paradigm shift for many. Crossing what could be construed as a second chasm may lead to the greatest aggregate improvement in the integration of sustainability initiatives and should be a catalyst for all firms to get started. While these practices may not be implemented evenly by all industries, those who choose to explore these environmental practices and DfS will find many opportunities to learn, differentiate, and for Innovators and Early Adopters, gain competitive advantage.

Given the inherent differences in how firms approach integrating sustainability into the product design process, there are a number of frameworks and tools that are available to help you cross the chasm in understanding and operationalizing DfS.

Summary

Our own work with companies integrating sustainability has shown a concern for what some have described as a "myopic focus on costs." While costs are important, Innovators and Early Adopters have been able to realize cost savings through better design, leveraging transportation, lengthening ROI and payback timelines on new projects, while leveraging the SVA of sustainability opportunities. This is important for several reasons as a firms focus will move from products, to processes and to packaging, you need to answer the question "how do we change processes to eliminate waste, or do we simply go after the outputs?" By understanding if your current efforts are process or output driven, you will be able to recognize opportunities to design proactively for more effective supply chain management.

By reading this two-volume set and purposefully setting aside some of your time to gain insight from a series of Action Items (AIs) and Audit Questions (AQs) found within each chapter, the end goal of this process should be a tailored approach to supply chain transformation. This transformation starts with an understanding of sustainable supply chains and their benefits before we go on to systematically assesses your own supply chain to help identify and execute sustainable practices. This assessment process will help develop a sustainable supply chain vision and strategy: create an executable plan for new sustainable supply chain projects; provide opportunities to integrate sustainable practices throughout your company, as well as among suppliers and customers; bring about better clarity regarding supply chain processes; leverage existing enterprise-resource-planning (ERP)-enabled manufacturing activities (energy consumption, emissions, scrap and waste, recycling, remanufacturing, packaging); guide you as to where to look for improvements in warehousing and fleet management; enable strategic sourcing highlighting the importance of design thinking, create programs for sustainable raw materials and packaging; and how to plan for closed-loop systems and reverse logistics activities, while leveraging existing systems and programs to identify and operationalize opportunities for existing and new sustainability practices.

Information within this book is sequenced in a way to help accomplish all of the aforementioned while taking the complex paradigm of sustainability and breaking it down into constituent parts focusing on how systems work. Chapters begin with evidence-based management, highlighting short vignettes, recent trends, and sustainability initiatives from innovative and early adopting firms. Information within chapters reveals applicable frameworks, tools, and proven standards as enablers of sustainable supply chain management (SSCM) initiatives. The end of each chapter challenges readers to reflect on their own operations through applied action-learning opportunities focusing the reader on AIs.

Applied Learning: Action Items (AIs)—Steps you can take to apply the learning from this chapter

AI: Where is your firm on the sustainability adoption model?

AI: Why is your firm considering sustainability?

AI: To what extent are your sustainability concerns driven by marketing or strategic needs?

AI: Do you have a formal design process in place?

AI: Who are the Innovators and Early Adopters of sustainability in the transportation industry?

AI: To what extent is sustainability integrated into your product design processes, or the processes of your customer?

AI: To what extent is sustainability integrated into the performance measurement system at the product level? Supply chain/supplier level?

Further Readings

Benyus, J. M. (1997). Biomimicry: Innovation Inspired by Nature, New York, NY: HarperCollins Publishers Inc..

Braungart, M., McDonough, W. (2007). Cradle to Cradle design: Creating Healthy Emissions—A Strategy for Eco-effective Product and System Design. *Journal of Cleaner Production.* 15(13–14): 1337–1348.

Ehrenfeld, J. R. (2008). *Sustainability by Design.* New Haven: Yale University Press.

Fiksel, J. (1996). *Design for Environment.* New York, NY: McGraw-Hill.

Moore, G. A. (2014). *Crossing the Chasm: Marketing and Selling Disruptive Products to Mainstream Customers* (3rd ed.). New York, NY: HarperCollins Business.

CHAPTER 2

Frameworks and Tools

Man is a tool-using animal. Without tools, he is nothing; with tools, he is all.

—Thomas Carlyle

As noted in the preceding chapter, the desire to be sustainable combined with management support (especially top management support), while important, is not enough. We need frameworks and tools. These important elements provide support to those charged with developing and deploying sustainable systems. Frameworks provide structure; they show the relationship between the various components and how these components can be arranged to generate more sustainable practices. Tools, on the other hand, provide the vehicle whereby specific tasks or goals can be achieved. They simplify problem solving, provide structure, and help guide and direct decision making. An important component of tools are the measures and metrics—tools that communicate the importance of sustainability and that help motivate people and organizations to achieve higher levels of sustainability performance. When used together, they result in new insight, cost savings, impact reduction, and differentiation as a result of leveraging sustainability for operations and supply chains. Examples include:

- The DuPont mission is "sustainable growth"—creating shareholder and societal value while reducing the company's footprint throughout the value chain. DuPont businesses leverage the role of life cycle assessment (LCA) in setting the goals, in developing innovative solutions for sustainable product and process design, in monitoring progress toward goals, and in stakeholder engagements.

- Timberland conducted an LCA for a leather boot and calculated emissions at all stages of the value chain, including sub-suppliers like the cattle industry that provided the leather. Surprisingly, leather use was responsible for most of the emissions, at around 80 percent of the boot's greenhouse gas (GHG) burden. Timberland now knows that reducing the amount of leather per boot will shrink its climate-change impact far more than reducing energy use at assembly plants or distribution centers.

- Data from companies such as Trucost enable organizations to identify, measure, and manage the environmental risk associated with their operations, supply chains, and investment portfolios. Quantifying environmental risks and a price for these risks is key to their approach. Entities like this one utilize public and proprietary data in providing a systematic approach to measuring and managing supply chain impacts leveraging data to quantify the environmental costs of suppliers, including carbon, water, waste, and air pollution.

Companies like DuPont, Timberland, and Trucost taken a deeper dive into understanding their products, processes, and supply chains. If you think no one has been watching, then you are wrong. Assessment enablers such as the Carbon Disclosure Project (CDP) and Trucost (acquired by the S&P Dow Jones Indices) are tracking and valuing these efforts while revealing how much waste and costs typically go unseen within supply chains. In this chapter, we continue the evolution of design trends, and help to operationalize integration. We will review important frameworks and tools such as the Framework for Strategic Sustainable Development (FSSD), Industrial Ecology, LCA, and C2C, before reviewing opportunities to design with less energy and materials with the integration of planning, and project assessment for products, packaging, and supply chains. We end the chapter with a look at the role of transportation providers.

Objectives

1. Build on the first chapter's design and transformational opportunities.
2. Review current frameworks and tools of sustainability.

3. Leverage a systems perspective, understand how to determine success, and find strategic integration opportunities within firms and supply chains.

To understand the importance of tools, consider the following story. Even though it deals with Quality Management, the lessons that it offers for those interesting in sustainability is profound:

Bill Conway, the former chairman of Nashua Corporation and an early champion of Total Quality Management (TQM) statistical methods, was host to a high-level delegation from Ford. The delegation wanted to probe the reasons for Nashua's quality success. Conway started the meeting with a challenge—"Suppose I ask two of you successful vice-presidents at Ford to enter a contest. The winner will win a trip around the world for his whole family. I know that both of you are totally motivated and dedicated by virtue of your exalted position at Ford. The contest is to see who can drive a nail into this wall. One you will get a hammer, the other nothing but management encouragement! How do you think will win?" The answer was obvious. Motivation is important, management encouragement is important, but employees at all levels must have tools. They must be the right tools.

What Bill Conway recognized was the critical importance of tools and frameworks. They provide the vehicle by which intent becomes realized, by which thought becomes concrete. While management support and organizational commitment are important, tools and framework are critical. They offer the foundation on which successful deployment and management are ultimately built. Therefore, before presenting the various tools and frameworks, it is first important to understand why these are so important to the attainment of effective sustainability.

Frameworks and Tools an Overview

Frameworks and tools are critical to the successful deployment of sustainability. They are critical because of the different roles that they play. Frameworks are broad based; they provide the users with a *road map* that links the various tools, programs and components together and to the goal—improved sustainability. Frameworks also provide *causality*—they show how the actions lead to the goal. In contrast, tools are instruments for helping personnel solve very specific issues or problems. They can be used to organize the data (with the goal of identifying patterns) or to flag areas to examine in detail. They can also be used to develop and deploy solutions.

When dealing with framework and tools, there are two points to remember:

First, for frameworks and tools to be actually used effectively, they must be understood and accepted by those using them. As Gene Woolsey, an operations researcher once noted, *"A person would rather live with a problem they can see than use a solution that they cannot understand."* Second, if the frameworks or tools are replacing existing procedures, then the existing approaches must first be discredited. There is a tendency to assume that people are adaptive thinkers. That is, if you teach them a new procedure, they will add it to the set that they currently have. Furthermore, we assume that they will use the tools if we first show them that the tools work and second we provide the users with a strong rationale for using them. The fact of the matter is that this view is wrong. People are substitutive rather than additive thinkers. They will use the current approaches and only those tools that fit with these current approaches UNTIL the current approaches are discredited—shown to be wrong or ineffective. Until this happens, the users will respond by offering the following:

- Lip service: Telling you that they do what you want them to do, even though they are not.
- Selective listening: Listening and applying only those tools and frameworks that fit with the existing approaches.
- Covering up through measures and metrics: Most personnel in a firm know that management will not go to the floor or to their areas and see what they are doing. They also know that measures are imperfect indicators of behaviors. Consequently, there is a potential for personnel to "game" the measures to hide what they are doing.

Available Frameworks and Tools to Help Cross the Chasm

Albert Einstein once said "the world that we have created today as a result of our thinking thus far has problems that cannot be solved by thinking the way we thought when we created them." The new way of thinking about the opportunities that comes from environmental and social issues starts with Design for Sustainability (DfS) and design thinking and extents throughout the supply chain, and becomes part of an integrated approach to the innovation process. To help in this process, we draw from several frameworks and tools to help the product development process. Some of the leading approaches that allow managers to see the world through a more sustainable lens include the FSSD (formerly known as The Natural Step), C2C design, industrial ecology, natural capital, biomimicry, and LCA.

Framework for Strategic Sustainable Development

The Natural Step (TNS: www.naturalstep.org) is an organization founded in Sweden in the late 1980s by the scientist Karl-Henrik Robèrt. Following publication of the Brundtland Report in 1987, Robèrt developed TNS framework,[1] proposing four system conditions for the sustainability of human activities on earth. Robèrt's system conditions are derived from the laws of thermodynamics, promote systems thinking, and set the foundation for how we can approach decision-making.

The first and second laws of thermodynamics set limiting conditions for life on earth: The first law says that energy is conserved; nothing disappears, but its form simply changes. The implications of the second law are that matter and energy tend to disperse over time. This is referred to as "entropy." Merging the two laws and applying them to life on earth, the following becomes apparent:

1. All the matter that will ever exist on earth is here now (first law).
2. Disorder increases in all closed systems and the Earth is a closed system with respect to matter (second law). However, it is an open system with respect to energy since it receives energy from the sun.

---

[1]Nattrass and Altomare (1999), Chapter 2.

3. Sunlight is responsible for almost all increases in net material quality on the planet through photosynthesis and solar heating effects. Chloroplasts in plant cells take energy from sunlight for plant growth. Plants, in turn, provide energy for other forms of life, such as animals. Evaporation of water from the oceans by solar heating produces most of the Earth's fresh water. This flow of energy from the sun creates structure and order from the disorder. So what does this have to do with business practices?

Taking into account the laws of thermodynamics, in 1989, Robèrt drafted a paper describing the system conditions for sustainability. After soliciting outside opinions and achieving scientific consensus, his efforts became TNS's system conditions of sustainability and what is now called the FSSD[2] and organization enabling this framework within cities and organizations, TNS Consultancy.

The Framework's definition of sustainability includes system conditions that lead to a sustainable society.

In this sustainable society, nature should *not* be subject to systematically increasing:

1. Concentrations of substances extracted from the Earth's crust.
2. Concentrations of substances produced as a byproduct of society.
3. Degradation by physical means.

And in that society, people are not subject to systematic social obstacles[3] to the following:

4. Health.
5. Influence.

---

[2]Broman, G. I., & Robert, K. H. (2017). A framework for strategic sustainable development. *Journal of Cleaner Production.*

[3]These social sustainability dimensions are from the work of Merlina Missimer, Missimer M, Robért K-h, and Broman G. 2014. "Lessons from the field: A first evaluation of working with the elaborated social dimensions of the Framework for Strategic Sustainable Development". Presented at Relating Systems Thinking and Design 3, Oslo, 15-17 October 2014. Published as part of Merlina Missimer's doctoral dissertation series No. 2015:09, Blekinge Institute of Technology, Department of Strategic Sustainable Development, Karlskrona, Sweden 2015.

6. Competence.
7. Impartiality.
8. Meaning making.

Positioned instead as the principles of sustainability, to become a sustainable society, economy, industry, supply chain, business, or individuals, we must:

1. Eliminate our contribution to the progressive buildup of substances extracted from the earth's crust (e.g., heavy metals and fossil fuels).
2. Eliminate our contribution to the progressive buildup of chemicals and compounds produced by society (e.g., dioxins, Polychlorinated Biphenyl's (PCBs), dichlorodiphenyltrichloroethane (DDT), and other toxic substances).
3. Eliminate our contribution to the progressive physical degradation and destruction of natural processes (e.g., overharvesting forests, paving over critical wildlife habitat, and contributions to climate change).
4. Eliminate exposing people to social conditions that systematically undermine people's capacity to avoid injury and illness (e.g., unsafe working conditions, a nonlivable wage).
5. Eliminate exposing people to social conditions that systematically hinder them from participating in shaping the social systems they are part of (e.g., suppression of free speech, or neglecting opinions).
6. Eliminate exposing people to social conditions that systematically hinder them from learning and developing competencies individually and together (e.g., obstacles to education, or personal development).
7. Eliminate exposing people to social conditions that systematically imply partial treatment (e.g., discrimination, or unfair selection to job positions).
8. Eliminate exposing people to social conditions that systematically hinder them from creating individual meaning and co-creating common meaning (e.g., suppression of cultural expression, or obstacles to co-creation of purposeful conditions).

A review of your organization's practices and infractions of these sustainability principles is part of a baseline understanding where leaders and organizations should focus resources and efforts to bring about change. A five-level framework applied to planning and assessment can help any organization better determine why and how to approach change management initiatives. The five levels are the system, success, strategic, actions, and the use of tools.

At the **Systems level**, you need to understand the system in which you operate and the natural laws that define the biosphere and societies relationship with the biosphere. **Success** is based on the sustainability principles and outlines the minimum requirements necessary for success. The sustainability principles become the minimum and foundation for your operating manual. **Strategic** guidelines should guide decision-making processes. Using an ABCD planning process, backcasting from your vision of the future provides guidelines for socially sustainable processes of relating transparency, cooperation, openness, inclusiveness, and involvement.[4] **Actions** come from prioritized steps put into action while following strategic guidelines for success in the systems. Finally, applying the appropriate **Tools** incudes management techniques and monitoring processes to guide implementation of strategic planning.

In order to illustrate the issue of sustainability, the FSSD uses the image of a funnel to demonstrate how decreasing resource availability and increasing consumer demand on those resources will eventually intersect, leading to a breakdown of the system (Figure 2.1). If, however, a company moves toward designing and operationalizing regenerative products, processes and systems, resources and demand can continue forward on a sustainable path.

How can any firm or project team apply the FSSD? A simplified approach (much like Deming's Plan, Do, Check, Act) instead positions Awareness, Baseline, Create a Vision, and Down to Action to form the acronym ABCD, which describes the four steps of the framework to demonstrate its simplicity and its power.

---

[4]Sroufe, R. "Operationalizing Sustainability", *Journal of Sustainable Studies*, Issue 1.1, 2016.

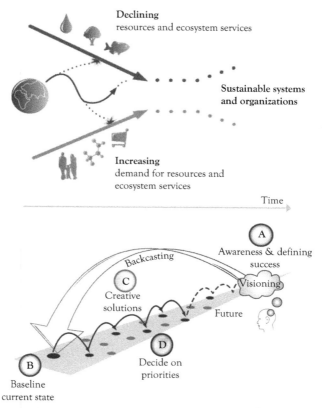

Figure 2.1 The FSSD funnel and ABCD application[5]

Source: Used with permission from TNS.

- *Awareness*: Work to create awareness of the idea of sustainability among stakeholders. Begin internally among managers, cross-functional teams and within function champions, include line workers, purchasing, and drivers of trucks. When ready, (meaning when you can demonstrate capabilities and alignment with your value proposition) create awareness externally by releasing information first to your key customer(s) and suppliers and then release this information publicly.
- *Baseline*: Take a close look at all aspects of operations, from stage-gate product design process, to management decision

---

[5]The Natural Step: http://www.naturalstep.org/

making and key performance indicators. Audit/benchmark current operations to understand the "as is" state and help determine the "to be" state and performance metrics. Include metrics such as GHG emissions, other forms of waste and social performance, transportation system design, supply chain practices, and employee and driver awareness.

- *Create a Vision*: Take what the baseline produced to see where you want to be in the future. Find opportunities for innovation. Set high goals. Define how you will measure success. From these goals, *backcast* to current operations and decision-making utilizing systems thinking to see how decisions today will or will not move you closer to the future vision.

- *Down to Action*: Prioritize and set goals. Assess projects and initiatives by asking if they take your firm toward or away from its vision. Make the business case for return on investment (ROI); is this a good sustainable value added (SVA)? Create a contingency plan to anticipate risk management factors such as regulatory and cost-structure changes.

By following this framework, whole communities such as Whistler British Columbia, Madison Wisconsin, and Santa Monica California have strategically integrated sustainability into their planning. Multinational corporations such as Nike and IKEA (to name a few) have applied it to operations. The application of strategic sustainable development lends itself well to integrating supply chains, and applied systems thinking to improve business model alignment of critical customers, capabilities, and value propositions. The result, a collective vision of the future, the use of tools including LCA, GHG Protocol, Environmental Management Systems, environmental and social metrics, and even integrated closed-loop systems to turn the vision into a reality. Next, we review other applicable frameworks and tools that help to integrate sustainability into strategic, tactical, and operational practices.

What follows is a brief case study to highlight how the FSSD can be applied to a firm, the integration opportunities for sustainability and extensions to sustainable supply chain management (SSCM).

Applying the FSSD to Aura Light's Supply Chain

Compiled by Velika Talyarkhan[6]

Aura Light, a sustainable lighting company, and Blekinge Institute of Technology (BTH) had a long-term consulting partnership which led to Aura Lighting changing its strategic direction. In 2009, Martin Malmos, Aura Light CEO, announced plans to make some major changes within the organization, based on BTH's introduction to the FSSD and the support of a specialist sustainability consultancy, TNS, has been a key part of Aura Light's new direction in developing a SSCM model with its suppliers. Aura Light's application of the FSSD's five-level framework for SSCM is outlined below[7]:

System level

The first step was to define the focus and boundaries of the work. To this end, the focal company would be Aura and its supply chain as a subsystem of the global society and biosphere. The boundary for SSCM is Aura Light, its supply chain, and consultants.

Success level

With the objective of understanding what success would look like, this level of application resulted in management and the organization wanting to do the following. Define a vision for each subsystem, and adhering to the eight sustainability principles of socioecological sustainability. One outcome was the following statement; "Aura Light's vision is to become the global leading partner for sustainable lighting solutions to professional customers."[8]

---

[6]Velika Talyarkhan, Graduate Assistant, Duquesne University MBA+Sustainability program.

[7]Bratt, Cecilia et al. "An introductory approach to strategic sustainable supply chain management." *Submitted for journal publicaiton* (2013)

[8]França, César, Bronman et al. "An approach to business model innovation and design for strategic sustainable development." *Journal of Cleaner Production* (2017): 155–166

- In this step, Aura Light identified the elements of its vision which would be driven by the SSCM function.
- SSCM success was defined as successfully and systematically eliminating all contributions to the supply chain which violate the eight principles. Potential SSCM goals included:
- Sustainable raw material sourcing.
- Optimized logistics and sustainable transport.
- A positive impact on local communities.
- No scarce materials or substances that risk increasing in concentration in nature.
- No health and safety risks.
- Share and develop competence in sustainability.
- Develop partnerships with customers, suppliers, communities, nongovernmental organizations, universities and governments.

Strategic guidelines level

Aligning with strategic plans for the organization was critical to success. Here they planned steps to achieve the defined success, defined the business case for sustainability, and balance the direction and speed of change with the ROI. SSCM strategic priorities include:

- Building trust and trustworthiness.
- Building deep collaboration.
- Effectively communicating the business case for sustainability.
- Committing to information exchange and transparency.
- Employing innovative thinking.
- Building competence for SSCM.
- Understanding and respecting local contexts.

Aura Light under TNS's guidance conducted a sustainable life cycle assessment (SLCA) for the company's two main products (fluorescent tube lights and long-life tube lights). As part of the SLCA, Aura Light mapped its suppliers and identified strategic players in the network through each life cycle process. The process included understanding the interrelatedness of all the supply chain actors, their geographic spread, and risks such as traceability of materials, competition and demand. In the future, other products that Aura manages, such as LED lights, will also require the SLCA to identify and manage risks and opportunities. At present, the baseline SCLA identified a lack of information on the following supply chain activities:

- Raw material extraction and processing.
- Production processes at suppliers.
- Transportation impacts (transport phase was not included in the assessment).

Following the supplier mapping, Aura Light plans to assess the gaps between its current state and desired sustainability vision. The development of a Strategic Supplier Sustainability Assessment tool can be used to identify existing hotspots in the supply chain such as:

- Do Aura Light's products contain scarce metals or persistent chemicals (contravening Sustainability Principles 1 and 2)?
- Are materials and energy used from sustainably managed ecosystems?
- Is any exposure to health hazards eliminated?
- Is a positive impact created on communities?

Actions level

At this level, they wanted to prioritize activities and develop an action plan for the achievement of the vision. External SSCM actions included joint workshops with suppliers and customers, along with training. Internal opportunities included co-creating supplier-specific product/service specifications, organizational objectives, targets and action plans.

Tools level

At this level they selected appropriate tools for enabling each level above, such as brainstorming, design-sprints, a business model canvas tool, diagnostic tools such as gap analysis, modeling and simulations, and quantitative LCA with supporting databases. A key tool for SSCM was the development of a Supplier Sustainability Assessment tool.

An example of a supplier sustainability assessment questionnaire is reproduced in Table 2.1, to illustrate the information required to assess supplier waste management practices and targets for social sustainable management of suppliers. ISO Quality Health Safety and Environment (QHSE) requirements could also provide a structure for developing a Supplier Sustainability Assessment tool.

Progress so far

Aura Light's sustainability goals have been mapped based on the new vision, and progress made accordingly, which is reported in an annual report. The goals below specifically relate to SSCM (Table 2.2).

Aura Light's application of the FSSD allows some insight into the integration of sustainability into supply chain management with known frameworks. This company's work is not complete as the use of the FSSD and ABCD planning process is an iterative approach that should be

Table 2.1 Prototype for Supplier Sustainability Assessment[8]

Aspect	Waste management
Desired	Waste is avoided, recycled, and/or reduced
Suggested question	Are the flows of waste monitored? Is it transparent where the flows of waste end-up? Are any waste management routines at hand? Are the production processes designed for recycling wherever it is applicable?
Aspect	Targets/action plans for social sustainable management of suppliers
Desired	Clear and co-developed targets and action plans for transparency and for sustainable supplier practices
Suggested question	Examples of questions for self-assessment of the focal company´s overall strategic approach: Has the focal company taken actions for transparency and for the co-development of targets and action plans to systematically deal with all social sustainability issues detected through a current status audit and the supplier strategic sustainability assessment?

---

[8]Bratt, Cecilia et al. "An introductory approach to strategic sustainable supply chain management." doctoral dissertation (2013)

Table 2.2 *2015 Sustainability Goals for Aura Light's Supply Chain*[9]

Success Factors	Focus goals (through 2015)	Results and operations 2015
Responsible business operations	• Our emissions of carbon dioxide will decrease in relation to our sales	• From now on we also climate compensate for inbound freights
	• More than 95% of the waste from production will be recycled	• Results 2015: 88%. Continued improvement in sorting efforts and materials used in production, which are now recycled.
	• 40% of chemicals containing substances from the prioritized substances for risk reduction (PRIO) list will be phased out	• Results 2015: 42% has been phased out.
	• The sustainability efforts of our main suppliers are evaluated and monitored through efficient processes	• Work with supplier audits is now an implemented process. Proposed measures from Aura Light dealt within a satisfactory way.

revisited often while also looking for other tools to help enable the transition to a more sustainable society and circular economy.

Eco-Effectiveness and Cradle to Cradle

Eco-effectiveness presents an alternative design and production concept to the strategies of zero emission and eco-efficiency.[10] Where eco-efficiency and zero emission seek to reduce the unintended negative consequences of processes of production and consumption, eco-effectiveness is a positive agenda for the conception and production of goods and services that incorporate economic, environmental, AND social benefit, enabling triple top line growth.

Eco-effectiveness moves beyond zero emission approaches by focusing on the development of products and industrial systems that maintain or enhance the quality and productivity of materials through subsequent life cycles. The concept of eco-effectiveness also addresses the major shortcomings of eco-efficiency approaches: their inability to address the necessity for fundamental redesign of material flows, their inherent antagonism

---

[9]Aura Light's 2015 Annual and Sustainability Report, http://np.netpublicator.com/netpublication/n97742801

[10]Braumguart and McDonough (2007), pp. 1337–1348.

toward long-term economic growth and innovation, and their insufficiency in addressing toxicity issues.

Cradle to cradle,[11] also called C2C, or sometimes interchangeable with "regenerative," is a biomimetic approach to the design of systems. Briefly discussed in Volume 1, Chapters 3 and 4, C2C models human industry on nature's processes in which materials are viewed as nutrients circulating in healthy, safe metabolisms. It suggests that industry must protect and enrich ecosystems and nature's biological metabolism while also maintaining safe, productive technical metabolism for the high-quality use and circulation of organic and synthetic materials. This design concept is a holistic economic, industrial, and social framework that seeks to create systems that are not just efficient but not detrimental to the people or the environment, and waste free. The model in its broadest sense is not limited to industrial design and manufacturing; it can be applied to many different aspects of human civilization such as urban environments, buildings, economics, and social systems.

A central component of the eco-effectiveness concept, C2C design provides a practical design framework for creating products and industrial systems in a positive relationship with ecological health and abundance, and long-term economic growth. Against this background, the transition to eco-effective industrial systems is a five-step process beginning with an elimination of undesirable substances. The steps involve the following:

1. Make sure a product is free of toxic substances.
2. Substitute personally preferred materials that are less hazardous.
3. Assessment of materials and classification as to their ability for biological metabolism—a passive positive list.
4. Optimization of the passive positive list identifying materials as either technical or biological nutrients—creating an active positive list of materials.
5. Reinvention of the relationship of the product and the customer— the product of service concept fits well with this.

---

[11]McDonough and Michael Braungart (2002). Also see, The Upcycle, the authors 2013 book from North Hill Press.

Eco-effectiveness ultimately calls for a reinvention of products by reconsidering how they may optimally fulfill the need or needs for which they are actually intended while simultaneously being supportive of ecological AND social systems. This process necessitates the creation of a system of materials management to coordinate material flows among processes and whole organizations in the product system. The concept of industrial ecology illustrates how such a system might take shape.

Industrial Ecology

Industrial ecology is an interdisciplinary field involving the relationships between industrial systems and their natural environment. Industrial systems may be conceived on a micro level as firms or industries or on a macro level as industrial societies. The industrial metabolism, that is, the flows of energy and materials through socioeconomic structures, is seen as the major driver of environmental burdens and threats to sustainability. Technology in its function of transforming energy and materials into goods and services, and inevitably also into wastes and emissions, is seen as a key to more sustainable solutions.

The term, industrial ecology, was popularized by Robert Frosch and Nicholas Gallopoulos.[12] Following the development of the framework, the field developed during the 1990s and has spawned academic programs, scholarly journals, and an international society. Industrial ecology draws on principles from thermodynamics, systems theory, and ecology. LCA, material flow accounting (MFA), and environmental input-output analysis are primary tools used in the field. Building on the notion of symbiosis in nature, highly interconnected industrial networks using wastes as process inputs (industrial symbioses) should more closely mimic the parsimony of closed-loop natural systems.

A famous example of industrial ecology in practice is an industrial district in the town of Kalundborg, Denmark. This small municipality has a well-developed network of dense firm interactions. The primary partners in Kalundborg, including an oil refinery, a power station, a gypsum board facility, and a pharmaceutical company, share ground water, surface

---

[12]Frosch and Gallopoulos (1989).

water, wastewater, steam, and fuel, and they also exchange a variety of by-products that become feedstocks in other processes. Successful outcomes of this industrial system includes 5 M liters of bioethanol produced annually, 19,500 tons of CO_2 are saved from using excess waste from the adjacent organizations, and 13,000 tons of lignin pellets have replaced coal at a power plant producing electricity and district heat for 5,000 area dwellings in Kalundborg city.[13]

Within this system, there are three primary opportunities for resource exchange: (a) Byproduct reuse—the exchange of firm-specific materials between two or more parties for use as substitutes for commercial products or raw materials. The materials exchange component has also been referred to as a byproduct exchange, byproduct synergy, or waste exchange, and may also be referred to as an industrial recycling network. (b) Utility/infrastructure sharing—the pooled use and management of commonly used resources such as energy, water, and waste water. (c) Joint provision of services—meeting common needs across firms for ancillary activities such as fire suppression, transportation, and food provision. High levels of environmental and economic efficiency have been achieved, leading to many other less tangible benefits involving personnel, equipment, and information sharing.

While in the early phase of this field, the focus was on technologies and firms and their interconnectedness, industrial ecology increasingly broadened its systemic perspective toward including production and consumption, trade and transportation, infrastructure, and lifestyles. Using industrial ecology to create a vision, the industrial transformation of entire economies, cities, industries, and supply chains can come into view.

Integrating Sustainability and Design: Life Cycle Assessment

The overlay of sustainability within supply chain analysis applies the emerging measurement tools and quantitative models that characterize various relationships and economic trade-offs in the supply chain. Supply chain analysis

---

[13]European Commission/European Research Area: Co-production of Bio-fuels (2013).

has made significant strides in both theoretical and practical applications of waste reduction. The application of a sustainability lens to analysis results in an unprecedented mixture of predictive models, and the ability to quantify environmental costs of operations, products, and whole supply chains.

LCA (see Figure 2.2) is a technique to assess the environmental aspects and potential impacts associated with a product, process, or service, by:

- Compiling an inventory of relevant energy and material inputs and environmental releases.
- Evaluating the potential environmental impacts associated with identified inputs and releases.
- Interpreting the results to help you make a more informed decision.

LCA is not a new tool, and has evolved over the last forty years. In the 1970s, companies in both the United States and Europe performed comparative life cycle inventory analyses. Inventory analysis is an objective, data-based process of quantifying energy and raw material requirements, air emissions, waterborne effluents, solid waste, and other environmental

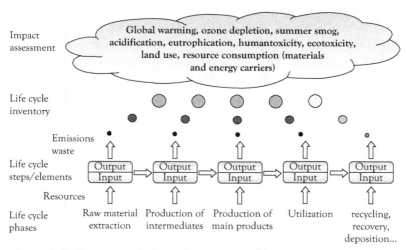

Figure 2.2 Overview of life cycle assessment[14]

Source: Used with permission from GaBi.

---

[14]PE International (2010).

releases incurred throughout the life cycle of a product, process, or activity. Much of the data was derived from publicly available sources such as government documents or technical papers, as specific industrial data were not available. The process of quantifying the resource use and environmental releases of products became known as a resource and environmental profile analysis (REPA), as practiced in the United States. In Europe, it was called an Ecobalance. The 1970s also saw the development of an economic input-output life cycle assessment (EIO-LCA) method theorized and developed by economist Wassily Leontief. The primary focus of this early period was the development of a protocol or standard research methodology for conducting these studies.

Through the early 1980s, life cycle inventory analysis continued and the methodology improved through studies focused on energy requirements. As interest in all areas affecting resources and the environment grew, researchers further refined and expanded the methodology beyond the life cycle inventory, to impact. Impact assessment refers to the phase of an LCA dealing with the evaluation of environmental impacts (e.g., global warming and toxicity) of products and services over their whole life cycle.

During the 1990s, false claims of environmental product attributes along with pressure from environmental organizations to standardize LCA methodology, led to the development of the LCA standards in the ISO 14000 series. Researchers at the Green Design Institute of Carnegie Mellon University operationalized Leontief's EIO-LCA method in the mid-1990s, with the help of sufficient computing power. This model is still available online taking the EIO-LCA method and transforming it into a tool available to quickly evaluate a commodity or service, as well as its supply chain.

After the turn of the century, the United Nations Environment Program (UNEP) joined forces with the Society of Environmental Toxicology and Chemistry (SETAC) to launch the life cycle initiative, an international partnership. The programs of the Initiative aim at putting life cycle thinking into practice and at improving the supporting tools through better data and indicators. The life cycle inventory (LCI) program improves global access to transparent, high-quality life cycle data by hosting and facilitating expert groups whose work results in web-based information systems. The life cycle impact assessment (LCIA) program increases the quality and global reach of life cycle indicators by promoting the exchange of views among experts whose work results in a set of widely accepted recommendations.[15] There are currently several proprietary software solutions to help make LCA a reality. The two most used in the United States and Europe are Simapro and GaBi, respectively.

Drill Down into Available Materials and Process Information

LCA quantifies the environmental impacts at each step of a product's life cycle. As a tool, LCA can be used to sustainably design products and even supply chains so that they have the least negative environmental impact.[16] Life cycle management (LCM) is the application of life cycle thinking to modern business practice, with the aim to manage the total life cycle of an organization's product and services toward more sustainable consumption and production.[17] It is an integrated framework of concepts and techniques to address environmental, economic, technological, AND social aspects of products, services, and organizations.

LCM is supported by environmental management systems and the ISO 14001 standards for these systems and research showing positive impacts on design, waste reduction, and recycling.[18] Additional resources are available online through the EPA, the National Services Center for Environmental Publications, and the Risk Management Sustainable Technologies websites. The benefits from these systems include proactive environmental management, resource and cost efficiency, enhanced reputation, and improved communication.[19] LCA-specific standards include ISO 14040 to 14044 as they describe the primary principles and framework for LCA including four primary steps:

1. Definition of the goal and scope of the assessment including system boundaries.
2. The life cycle inventory analysis phase.

---

[15]Scientific Applications International Corporation (SAIC), (2006).

[16]Ehrenfeld (2008).

[17]Jensen and Remmen (2006).

[18]Sroufe (2003).

[19]Curkovic and Sroufe (2011).

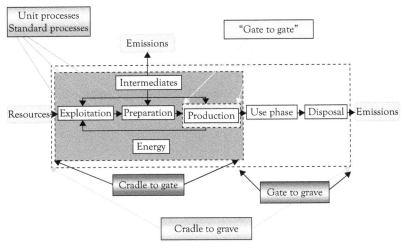

Figure 2.3 System boundaries

Source: Used with pemission from Gabi.

3. The life cycle impact assessment phase.
4. The life cycle interpretation phase, reporting and critical review of the assessment, limitations, and relationships between the four primary assessment phases.

Clarification of some terminology is needed to better understand LCA boundaries. Below are the main options to define the system boundaries used (shown in Figure 2.3):

Cradle to Grave: includes the material and energy production supply chain and all processes from the raw material extraction through the production, transportation, and use phases up to the product's end-of-life treatment.

Cradle to Gate: includes all processes from raw material extraction through the production phase (gate of the factory); used to determine the environmental impact of the production of a product.

Gate to Grave: includes the processes from the use and end-of-life phases (everything postproduction); used to determine the environmental impacts of a product once it leaves the factory.

Gate to Gate: includes the processes from the production phase only; used to determine the environmental impacts of a single production step or process.

Cradle to Cradle: includes the material and energy production supply chain and all processes from the raw material extraction through the production, transportation, and use phases before the product goes back into transportation closing the supply chain loop becoming a material used again in production, transportation, and use.

Clearly understanding the goal, scope, and system bounds allows LCA to be used as a tool to measure and track a product's resource use and impacts from cradle to grave, from raw material extraction to end-of-life processes. This tool is essential for managing sustainability risks, reducing waste and discovering opportunities to create environmentally and socially driven value. An established approach to a macro level of analysis involves systems thinking. This holistic approach to analysis focuses on the way that a system's constituent parts interrelate and how systems work over time and within the context of larger systems.[20] Conducting an LCA is one way to understand interconnected supply chain systems of products and services. The outcomes of an LCA lend themselves to supporting the ISO 14025 standard for environmental product labels and declarations.

A cradle-to-grave LCA allows a decision maker to study an entire product system and supply chain hence avoiding the suboptimization that could result if only a single process were the focus of the study. Stonyfield Farms in New Hampshire conducted an LCA on their yogurt product-delivery system to compare options for containers. Knowing the size of the container and the distance to retailer were important factors impacting the environment, they found that if they sold all of their yogurt in 32-ounce (0.95 liters) containers, they could save the equivalent of 11,250 barrels of oil per year. Transportation to the retailer represented about a third of their products' energy impact.[21]

---

[20]Meadows (2008).

[21]Branchfeld and Dov et al. (2001).

At 3M, the protocol for new product development includes assessment of environmental, health, and safety issues at suppliers, within 3M, and with the customer. This approach to understanding full-system impacts of its products gives 3M a foundation for building strategies leveraging an eco-advantage. Similar initiatives are taking place at companies such as Alcoa, Bayer, Dow, DuPont, and PPG where teams of LCA experts are now plugged into cross-functional teams in design and supply chain management. Resource efficiency and LCA become tools for pollution reduction and waste minimization allowing managers to better understand where they can have the most impact on a design, process, and supply chain.

Design Better Products, Packaging, and Supply Chains

Good managers know it's important to scan their external environment. They now look for the eco and social consequences of their products all along the value chain, upstream and downstream. Supply chain analysis tools and methods to integrate sustainability are most effective when they rest on a foundation of good data, careful planning, and an environment management system. Companies are now managing worldwide databases of sustainability performance metrics. Establishing key metrics such as GHG emissions that track results on energy use, water and air pollution, waste generation, and compliance help decision-makers benchmark performance, optimize supply chains, set goals, and monitor progress.

Closing the Loop

We should stop throwing away billions of dollars of valuable recyclable packaging materials. According to a report highlighting how the United States' lagging packaging recycling rates result in serious market inefficiencies and unnecessary strain on the economy and environment.[22] Packaging comprises over 40 percent of the U.S. solid waste stream, greater than any other category, and most of the materials are recyclable. Findings in the report include an estimate that the value of wasted recyclable consumer

---

[22]King (2012).

packaging materials exceeded $11 B and how extended producer responsibility (EPR) can lead to profits in processing used materials, reductions in carbon emissions and energy used to produce packaging, and thousands of jobs in within closed-loop supply chains for collection and processing. Further information from McKinsey finds manufacturers can create value, cut costs, and reduce exposure to volatile commodity prices by improving their resource productivity—using fewer resources for each unit of output.[23] Leaders are looking for opportunities beyond their own operations. Collaboration with suppliers and customers can keep used products, components, and materials in circulation while creating upwards $380 B (USD) of potential annual net material cost savings within the Europe. New business models that rethink the concept of ownership can shift value within closed-loop systems.

"Americans throw away more materials than any other country," said Conrad MacKerron, author of the report. "This used to be a sign of economic progress, but in an age of declining natural resources, such waste is now an indicator of inefficient use of valuable raw materials and market failure. It's simply not good business to throw away billions of dollars of reusable resources."

Information within the report outlines why companies should design closed-loop systems and take responsibility for postconsumer packaging as part of their ongoing sustainability policies. Packaging represents an overlooked system and industrial ecology opportunities because raw materials, such as the petroleum, minerals, and fiber used to make much consumer packaging, are projected to become increasingly scarce. The authors of the report also find that efficiently designed and administered EPR policies would resolve many of the concerns identified with packaging recycling by turning to the actions found in Figure 2.4.

- Increasing recovery rates for all postconsumer packaging.
- Incentivizing producers to reduce materials use and improve recyclability.
- Creating profitable secondary materials markets.

---

[23]McKinsey and Co. (2012).

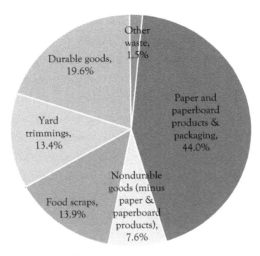

Figure 2.4 Percentage of solid waste steam

- Providing stable revenue sources through producer fees to improve curbside recycling systems and build new recycling infrastructure.
- Reducing energy consumption and GHGs.
- Meeting pent-up industry demand for recyclable materials.

A group of major consumer goods and grocery companies, including Colgate-Palmolive, General Mills, Kraft Foods, Safeway, Supervalu, Target, Kroger, Procter & Gamble, Unilever, Walmart, Whole Foods, Coca-Cola, and Nestlé Waters, are already working on solutions to help adopt EPR policies. By supporting the design of EPR policies that drive more aggressive and effective collection efforts, companies can then make commitments to use far higher levels of recycled content in product packaging, which, in turn, supports closed-loop systems ensuring a stable supply of postconsumer materials to use as new feedstock.

Why this is relevant to supply chain design and management? Does it only mean there is now more work for everyone? To answer the first question, supply chain professionals should have a seat at the design table and new sustainability projects. Supply chain insight should be involved early and often in the stage-gate new product development (NPD) process and work with the growing ranks of sustainability professionals.

With the increased focus on energy reduction initiatives within buildings, energy conservation thinking should be extended to transportation
systems, moving more goods with fewer resources and minimizing fuel
consumption.

To answer the second question, no, everyone does not have more
work, but instead this is an opportunity to quickly move up the learning curve on sustainability and realize we all can reimagine products,
processes, and systems. This is not more work, but a different way of
approaching the work you already perform. Each one of us can find and
eliminate waste, improve the business model, and rethink the way we
design with key customers in mind. There are already available, proven
approaches to help organize and focus on the integration of sustainability within existing processes. Systems thinking, stage-gate NPD processes, FSSD, Industrial Ecology, and C2C design all enable us to see
the world as dynamic and interrelated rather than static and limited to
functional siloes.

Companies overlooking the opportunity to manage sustainability and
closed-loop systems face risk from investors. In 2002, the CDP Project
surveyed and requested carbon information from the Financial Times
500 largest companies with only a 10 percent response rate. By 2005,
the response rate increased to 60 percent of the same companies surveyed.[24] Now, >80 percent of the Financial Times submit annual carbon
footprint reports. With the exponential growth in sustainability reporting and the integration of financial and sustainability reports, there will
be an increase in the development of material database that includes information on suppliers and where all components and parts come from
a given product. Increased supply chain transparency has already led to
open source, online LCA collaboration platforms such as Sourcemap.com
where anyone can see exactly where a product comes from, what kind of
environmental impacts materials have from extraction, to transportation
to the retail location, and delivery to your home.

The benefits are already be seen by some innovative firms such as
DuPont. At the turn of the century, forward-thinking leaders pledged
to cut carbon emissions 65 percent below their 1990 levels and to

---

[24]Read (2007).

accomplish this by 2010. The company reduced its emissions 67 percent while the value of DuPont stock increased 340 percent. By 2007, they had reduced company emission 80 percent below 1990 levels. These same efforts saved the company $3 B between 2005 and 2010. How much money can your organization save from cutting carbon emissions?

Role of Transportation Providers

Transportation service providers should see sustainability as a way to efficiency and productivity and manage transportation and logistics functions for their customers while also being considered early in the product design process. Sustainability allows the transportation and logistics function of any firm to create value by working with customers at a strategic level and by backing decisions with very detailed data from the product design process and application of LCA tools. While the business case for new initiatives often come as band aids and incremental improvement, combining sustainability and design thinking provides opportunities to leapfrog chasms and possibly cross the largest chasm between the Early Majority and Early Adopters.

When it comes to DfS product applications, the possibilities are limitless, but we realize that your time is not. The best approach is to assemble teams to get up to speed on sustainability initiatives within your industry. Then, perform gap analysis and review internal needs. Create a vision and set high sustainability goals, review the possible solution sets available through DfS, and backcast into current decision making. The use of teams and looking at the world through a design thinking lens will allow many to more quickly integrate sustainability into practice and performance metrics, and make timely proposals to improve efficiency and productivity.

Solutions can include a design focus on a spectrum of opportunities that include but are not limited to: shipment scheduling (interplant, inbound, and outbound), mode and mode-mix selection, optimization, carrier network development and management, transportation planning, load tendering, tracking and tracing, claims processing, freight bill payment, returns management, benchmarking, and reporting.

However, new initiatives demand products, processes, and solutions that are more practical, that is, more user-friendly, easily implemented, and less disruptive to existing systems. Sustainability is too often positioned in terms of new metrics. Thus, management needs to understand trade-offs, managing to what's critical and not doing everything at once. One way to approach this is to look for solutions that are designed to be:

- Proactive, understanding your business model and how you compete relative to others in your industry.
- Effective, allowing you to get more total product movement for less total cost.
- Evenhanded, not choosing one solution over another solely due to sustainability, but instead focus on the best solution for your business model.
- Realistic, effectively operationalized and understandable in existing financial terms.

Original equipment manufacturers (OEMs) and retailers value their relationships with transportation providers and recognize that they can reduce the impact of product movement. Key customers will look for their transportation partners to evaluate and minimize their fuel costs, environmental impacts, and increase social value by:

- Retrofitting existing vehicle fleets with technologies that increase fuel efficiency.
- Implementing process and practice changes to reduce fuel consumption.
- Training drivers in fuel-efficient driving techniques.
- Replacing existing inefficient vehicles with new, high-efficiency vehicles and technologies.
- Redesigning products and packaging to increasing packing rates with opportunities for closed-loop systems and recycling.
- Paying living wages to supply chain members.
- Including supply chain members in their ability to influence decision making, while also being informed as to what options are available and why changes are being made.

Environmental Protection Agency's ('EPA) SmartWay program (pre-viously described in Volume 1, Chapter 3) provides resources, educational content, and financing for making more fuel-efficient transportation a reality and is a logical resource for modernizing your own fleet, or under-standing what fuel-efficient practices you should expect from transporta-tion providers.

Other Tools and Procedures

In addition to these tools and frameworks, it should be noted that the var-ious tools and procedures developed for TQM can also be readily applied to sustainability. These include tools such as:

- Cause and Effect Analysis
- Pareto Charts
- P-D-C-A
- Control Charts
- Histograms
- Benchmarking

The advantage of applying these tools is that that they are widely accepted and there are numerous software packages for them.

Summary

Frameworks and tools are important. They explain; they provide tem-plates for success; they structure thinking. In this chapter, we have identified and explored several different frameworks and tools that are uniquely suited to the challenge of deploying effectively sustainability within the organization and its supply chain. Aura Light is but one example of the integration of sustainability within supply chain manage-ment. The application of the FSSD within your own organization and supply chain can change the way you think about, measure, and manage results. We have shown that for the manager willing to undertake this journey there are a wide range tools available—tools that need to be introduced and used.

Applied Learning: Action Items (AIs)—Steps you can take to apply the learning from this chapter

AI: Identify and assess the current sets of tools and frameworks being used in your organization. To what extent are these tools and frameworks consistent with the goals of sustainability?

AI: To what extent is sustainability and sustainability-related issues embedded in the current problems and issues being addressed by your company? Is sustainability an issue that is measured and where the consequences are suitably rewarded (or punished)?

AI: Assess the familiarity of your organization and its personnel with the various and framework identified in this chapter.

AI: If sustainability is new initiative that is different from the current areas being emphasized, have you developed a strategy for discrediting the current approaches?

AI: Can you find opportunities for LCA and industrial ecology within your operations and supply chain??

AI: To what extent are there frameworks in the organization that provide the personnel with a clear road map that links where the organization is currently with where it needs to be in the future?

AI: To what extent do the personnel see a clear and compelling reason for sustainability?

AI: Do the personnel understand the types of problems to which the various tools are most suitable? Least suitable?

AI: To what extent are the following options considered in your organization (product/process redesign, LCA, disassembly, substitution, reduce, recycle, remanufacture, consumer internally, waste segregation, alliances)?

Further Readings

Christensen, J., Park, C., Sun, E., Goralnick, M., Iyengar, J. (2008). A Practical Guide to Green Sourcing. *Supply Chain Management Review.* 12(8).

Global Environmental Management Institute (GEMI) (1993). *Total Quality Environment Management: The Primer.* Washington, DC: GEMI.

McDonough, W., & Braungart, M. (2002). Cradle to cradle: Remaking the Way We Make Things. New York: North Point Press.

McDonough, W., Braungart, M., & Clinton, B. (2013). The upcycle: Beyond sustainability—designing for abundance. Macmillan.

Works Cited

Bratt, C., et al. (2013). An Introductory Approach to Strategic Sustainable Supply Chain Management. *Submitted for journal publicaiton*

França, C., Bronman, G., et al. (2017). An Approach to Business Model Innovation and Design for Strategic Sustainable Development." *Journal of Cleaner Production*, 155–166.

Emerging Issues in Sustainable Supply Chain Management

CHAPTER 3

Integration

Supply Chain Management and Sustainability

Scope 3 emissions are a treasure map of opportunities across the value chain.

—Pankaj Bhatia, Director of the GHG Protocol,
at the Word Resources Institute

- In a recent report, the McKinsey and Company (Bové & Swartz, 2016) observed that the next 10 to 15 years will represent major opportunities for consumer companies, with some 1.8 billion people expected to join the global consuming class by 2025. Yet, this report noted that one factor that can significantly and adversely impact the firm's ability to take advantage of this unprecedented growth is poor sustainability performance—performance that begins in the supply chain. Failure to focus on the supply chain can affect financial performance, strategic objectives, and corporate reputations.[1]
- In 2014, the Global RepTrak® 100 ranking of the world's 100 most reputable companies included eight apparel companies. Of those,

---

[1] McKinsey and Company (Bové & Swartz, 2016), Starting at the source: Sustainability in supply chains.

two were dropped from the 2015 rankings[2]—the reason—their supply chains had, at the second- or third-tier level, outsourced from suppliers located in the Rana Plaza factory in Bangladesh. This factor had collapsed on April 24, 2013—killing 1,137 out of 3,639 workers—workers who did not want to enter the plant but were forced to when the owner, Sohel Rana, brought in paid gang members to beat the workers and to force them to enter the plant. These companies were left off the list in 2016.[3]

- Working with a panel of executives and external experts, including BSR, Conservation International, Food Animal Initiatives, and World Wildlife Fund, McDonalds now publishes a Best of Sustainable Supply Chain report highlighting supply chain partners working to improve food sources, the environment, communities, and employee wellness around the world. The best suppliers are recognized based on their measureable results and innovation.[4]

So far, our focus has been on the firm in isolation. By focusing on the firm alone, we overlook the importance of the structure that supports the firm. That is like us going to a game and watching a very successful team, without realizing that the success seen on the field is due in large part to the support of the processes and systems the team created. This support takes many forms—training, scouting, and talent development, to name a few. In today's business world, this support increasingly comes from the supply chain. That is, sustainability in the firm requires sustainability in the supply chain. This reality can be readily seen in the experiences of firms like McCormick & Company.

---

[2]2015 Global RepTrak® 100; https://www.reputationinstitute.com/CMSPages /GetAzureFile.aspx?path=~%5Cmedia%5Cmedia%5Cdocuments%5C2015-global-csr-reptrak-results.pdf&hash=f375854351576541ae88db1e043e7417e9f057f83 955bb3768454dd8e0417353&ext=.pdf

[3]2016 Global RepTrak® 100; https://www.rankingthebrands.com/PDF/Global%20 RepTrak%20100%20Report%202016,%20Reputation%20Institute.pdf

[4]McDonalds Corp. (2012).

McCormick & Company Achieves Sustainability Through Their Supply Chains

McCormick & Company is a multinational manufacturer, marketer, and distributor of spices, herbs, seasonings, specialty foods, and flavors to the food industry. From field to fork, this company has a history of sustainability and integration. Headquartered in Maryland, McCormick consists of over 13 major brands including McCormick U.S. Consumer Products, McCormick for Chefs, Industrial Flavor Solutions, Zatarain's, Simply Asia, McCormick Canada, Swartz, Ducros (France), Silvo (Netherlands), Margao (Spain and Portugal), and Vahine. Being an agriculture-based business, McCormick has long recognized that it is dependent on its suppliers for quality inputs into its business model and value creation process. More importantly, it is dependent on having a supply chain that is sustainable from both an environmental and a social perspective. To that end, McCormick has implemented a series of programs aimed at developing a growing, global supply chain that can support McCormick's needs both now and into the future. Among the programs introduced are the following:

- McCormick's Supplier Diversity Program—a program that seeks to develop relationships with qualified diverse businesses that are capable of meeting McCormick's quality needs while McCormick also provides assistance to improve economic conditions to the communities that supply their raw materials.
- Aggressive Global Sourcing—The company's Global Sourcing team works with local farmers to ensure that they follow best practices for growing crops at the local level. Since most spices can only be grown in certain specific areas and climates, McCormick works on building and maintaining a consistent and reliable supply of high-quality products. As an example, McCormick was an early and aggressive participant in Uganda's vanilla industry. It worked with aid agencies and nongovernmental organizations to improve quality, increase yield, and secure fair prices for the local farmers. The result of this long-term process was an established demand for high-quality vanilla combined with jobs for local farmers that paid

a living wage. Similar activities have been undertaken in India and Indonesia.

- Strict Adherence to a Companywide Supplier Code of Conduct— McCormick established a standardized internal compliance system to maintain strict high-quality standards worldwide.
- Transparency in the Supply Chain—A practice that enabled McCormick to meet and exceed the strict requirements of the recently introduced California Transparency in Supply Chain Act of 2010—an act that went into effect on January 1, 2012. This act aimed to increase the amount of information made available by manufacturers and retailers regarding their efforts to address the issue of slavery and human trafficking.

In short, in McCormick, we see a company that has had to rely on its supply chain for more than simply product—it is dependent upon its supply chain to provide consistently high-quality products grown in a sustainable manner and that are free of problems such as child labor, slavery, and human trafficking. To McCormick, the effective supply chain is the key to successful sustainability.

Objectives

When it comes to sustainability, there is no way that any firm can escape one central truth—you are no stronger or better than your weakest link. In a world where supply chain management is a given, not an option, this means that you are no better than the weakest link in your supply chain. Therefore, sustainability must become a supply chain mandate, not simply an internal mandate. This issue forms the central core of this chapter.

By the end of this chapter, you will be able to:

1. Understand the integrated supply chain is and such tactics as supplier base management and interoperability.
2. Review the drivers, barriers, and enablers associated with integrating the supply chain into corporate sustainability initiatives.
3. Apply a systematic approach to making sustainability a day-to-day habit.

As we can see from McCormick, supply chains are critical to sustainability. However, this insight is not new nor is it limited to the food products industry. In Chapter 3, we began our journey into sustainability by describing the changes now taking place at Unilever, where Paul Polman was implementing a new direction for this very successful company. If you examine the key strategic initiatives, you find the supply chain playing a central role. Polman did not simply see the new key customers being drawn from developing countries; he also saw these same markets as being the suppliers—growing products in a sustainable fashion for Unilever. This strategy impacts Unilever in two ways. First, Unilever, like McCormick, now has a secure, sustainable supplier base that is able to support the strategic goals and aims of Unilever. Second, by developing this supplier base, and by paying them a living wage, Unilever, like McCormick, has helped create community infrastructure and a new set of customers—people who are now able and willing to buy the products offered by companies such as McCormick and Unilever.

This recognition of the importance of the supply chain to the success of sustainability is not limited to companies such as Unilever and McCormick. Others have also recognized the importance of the supply chain to sustainability—companies such as Walmart, McDonald's, Nestlé, Intel, Novozymes (a producer and seller of industrial enzymes, microorganisms, and biopharmaceutical ingredients), Procter & Gamble, and Coca-Cola (to name a few) have also come to this same realization. That is, in today's business environment, the supply chain is critical; to succeed with sustainability, the supply chain must play a major role. The rest of this chapter explores the role played by the integrated supply chain in sustainability.

Supply Chain Management—A Synopsis

Supply chain management can be viewed as the design and execution of relationships and flows that connect the parties and processes across a supply chain. Supply chains, as illustrated in Figure 3.1, consist of both upstream (from our firm back through our suppliers ultimately to the source of the raw materials) and downstream (from our firms through the various customers to the ultimate customer—the consumer). Understanding how these activities work together, the business models and performance

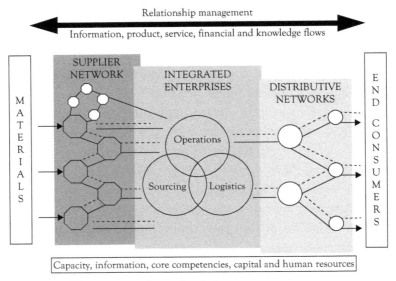

Figure 3.1 The integrated supply chain

measurement behind them, how information flows in both directions, and how they can be integrated is important to improving the supply chain. As indicated by the definition, supply chain management includes both relationships and flows.

Relationships deal with the types of linkages that are built between partners in the supply chain. We could have close, collaborative relationships, characterized by frequent contact between partners and constant sharing of information and risk. Alternatively, we can have arm's length relationships. In these relationships, we have limited sharing of information and our contacts are limited to the placing and receiving of orders and the resolution of any problems associated with these orders. Flows, as shown in Figure 3.1, consist of processes used to design, supply, produce and deliver valuable goods and services to customers.

Supply Chain Management—Benefits and Risks

Supply chain management has emerged as a major business paradigm for several reasons. Understanding this paradigm is critically important to finding where and how sustainability initiatives will fit within existing systems.

First, the supply chain enables the firm to respond quickly to customers whose needs are dynamically and continuously changing. With the old approach (i.e., pre-supply chain management), when demand changed, the firm would have to change its capacities. This, in turn, defined its capabilities, or what the firm could and could not do. To change capacities, it would have to build capacity and/or hire more people. All of these actions took time and exposed the firm to potential risk (e.g., of increasing capacity only to find that the demand was not sufficiently persistent). With supply chain management, firms now realize that they can rely on their suppliers when responding to changes in demand. This flexibility not only applies to capacity but also capabilities (specific skills that we need to meet the changing requirements of the business model). As the required capabilities change, we can turn to our supply chain to look for these new capabilities. This strategy reduces response time, costs, and potential risks.

Second, by turning to our suppliers, we can rationalize investments and focus. No firm can do everything well. Furthermore, some skills are important to our strategies and to our customers while others are not. These critical skills are referred to as core capabilities. For example, Honda's core capabilities lie in its ability to design and manufacture an efficient, low-vibration engine. Every product or business line that Honda enters is characterized by its demand for such an engine—cars, motorcycles, lawn mowers, snow blowers, generators, marine engines, and now jet engines. Consequently, it makes sense for the firm to focus on its core capabilities and to outsource everything else (ideally to those having the appropriate core capabilities in these outsourced products). Furthermore, by identifying the core capabilities, any organization can develop a firm rule for what is never outsourced—your core capability. By involving the supply chain, firms can focus on becoming better on their core capabilities. Third, by involving our suppliers and customers directly through supply chain management, the firm can draw on their insights, expertise, and problem-solving skills. This means that better solutions can be identified much more quickly and at lower costs.

Finally, we must recognize that products and information flow both ways in the supply chain. The same supply chain that brings goods and services to the market can also be used to manage the collection, disposal, and recycling of products that have reached the end of their useful life. This reverse flow goes under several different names, for example, reverse logistics or product take back (this development will be discussed in greater detail later on in this chapter). This is what we see being done by McDonald's UK, where the company uses the same trucks that deliver new goods to their restaurants to also collect cardboard for recycling. This practice has significantly reduced the amount of waste going to landfill as well as lessening emissions from transport. In 2010, McDonald's UK diverted 12,000 tons of cardboard from landfill sites to recycling facilities.[5]

Yet, against these important advantages, supply chain management does expose the firm to certain problems. First, with supply chain management, there is the issue of lack of control. Since you are now working with suppliers who are not owned by your firm, this means that you are dependent on them to work in a manner that is consistent with the dictates of your business model. This is a critical issue for firms where sustainability is core to their business model.

For example, the supply chains in some industries (including electronics, textiles, cocoa, and coffee), which involve developing countries, are plagued by human rights and health and safety violations. Human rights issues include excessive overtime, low wages, unsafe working conditions, and even forced and child labor. Unless addressed, the responsibility for these problems will be laid at the feet of the firm in whose supply chain these problems occur. Not knowing that these problems are taking place does not protect the firm from being blamed. For instance, in 2012, an audit supported by Nestlé found violations of its labor code of conduct, including the use of child labor by suppliers in the Ivory Coast, which is the world's largest producer of cocoa. Stating that eliminating child labor in its supply chain is its number one priority, Nestlé is collaborating with the Fair Labor Association to train and certify suppliers, increase monitoring, and work with the Ivory Coast government.

Closely associated with the preceding point, there is the issue of lack of visibility. As we proceed further and further away into the supply

---

[5]King (2012).

chain (into lower and lower tiers—from tier 1 to tier 2 to tier 3), we begin to lose visibility into what is happening at these lower levels. Consequently, like Nestlé, we may find ourselves faced by problems created at lower levels that can adversely affect our performance. This lesson has been painfully driven home to Mattel Toys. In August 2007, Mattel, America's largest toy manufacturer, announced the first of five recalls involving 21 million toys (most of which were made in China), with the recalls taking place from August to November. The source of these recalls is problems created within the third tier of Mattel's supply chain.

In many cases, the problems created at one level are often hidden as the products move through the various levels until they reach the final stage. Once they get there, the problems become evident—often too late for the firm to do anything about them.

It was noted earlier that the problems of visibility and control are essentially important when dealing with sustainability. The reason is that once a firm decides to compete on sustainability as its primary core value, then the marketplace holds the firm accountable not only for its performance but also for the performance its supply chain partners. The responsibility for problems in the supply chain is often directly assigned to that party that is most visible in the supply chain. This lesson has been painfully learned by companies such as the Body Shop, Apple (with its supplier—Foxconn and that supplier's history of labor management problems and violations of child labor laws), and Nestlé.

Finally, by relying on the supply chain, we create the possibilities that we may be adversely affected by problems within the supply chain. That is, a disruption at the supplier level for whatever reason (e.g., bankruptcy, labor strike, or natural disaster such as tsunami, earthquake, or fire) combined with a lack of adequate protection (in the form of excess inventory, excess capacity, or excess lead time) can result in stockouts and production problems at the firm.

As can be seen from this discussion, supply chain management is a dual-edged sword. It is becoming a necessary fact of life; it brings with it certain critical advantages; it also brings with it certain risks and potential problems. Yet, for sustainability, integrated supply chain management is a necessity for success.

The Rise and Current State of Sustainable Supply Management

Our own research based on interviews with sustainability executives from large multinational corporations (including 3M, Alcoa, Baxter, Dow, DuPont, EMC, FedEx Ground, Ford, Johnson & Johnson, H.J. Heinz, Herman Miller, IBM, and P&G to name a few) provides insight as to how they operationalized sustainability internally and work with supply chain managers to integrate supply chains.[6] When asked how management knows if they are successful in meeting objectives for sustainability and its integration, we find the following top three primary areas of focus for these executives involves: performance measurement; the importance of rankings; and the development of sustainability reports.

As we know from Volume 1 and our own insights, performance measurement is a key enabler of sustainability. When discussing the importance of measurement, the majority of participants highlighted setting goals and key performance indicators (KPIs) as the most important enablers of understanding if operations and processes are progressing toward sustainability goals. It was noted that "compliance" is something applied to regulation and known standards. Instead of looking at environmental regulations, sustainability should be everyone's responsibility and demonstration of this can be found in meeting and exceeding goals while tracking KPIs. What makes new initiatives successful is a combination of leadership, short-term and long-term projects, a road map, and compensation tied to performance of natural AND social capital initiatives. While there are many different metrics discussed by MNCs we worked with, the most frequently noted include the following:

1. Energy efficiency.
2. Greenhouse gas (GHG) emissions.
3. Water consumption.
4. Solid waste.
5. Product attributes.
6. Environmental exposure.

---

[6]Sroufe et al. (2012).

7. Benchmarking up to multiple environmental and sustainability indices.
8. Carbon indexed to products and revenue.

The importance of rankings cannot be overlooked. Something on the minds of managers everywhere includes the following, "how is success/compliance with sustainability measured?" The response to this question by executives and managers from the companies we have worked with demonstrates the importance of the external evaluation of a company as a measure of the integration of sustainability within a firm and within its supply chain. Some approaches to external scanning captures and looks for competitors or their own firm's inclusion within upwards of 15 separate environmental and sustainability rankings annually. Inclusion within a ranking is leveraged by sustainability professionals to validate practices and demonstrate programs going beyond compliance. The three primary rankings or indices highlighted in this study, in order of frequency are Newsweek's Green Rankings, the Carbon Disclosure Project (CDP), and the Dow Jones Sustainability Index with the Davos rankings also garnering attention. Managers expressed frustration with the difficulties in understanding the meaning of sustainability as there are different ranking methodologies used across industries. There is a need for commonly accepted methodologies for measuring and assessing sustainability indices and rankings. One commonly recognized approach is with the use of the global reporting initiative (GRI) outlined in Volume 1, Chapter 3.

The GRI is highlighted as the leading approach to measuring and disclosing information. Other important highlights include the use of integrated financial, environmental, AND social reporting, and the ISO certification also demonstrating assurance of performance within known standards. To this end, environmental management systems (ISO 14001) continue to be important enablers of measuring and managing performance. These management systems are a formal system and database that integrate procedures and processes for the training of personnel, monitoring, summarizing, and reporting of specialized environmental performance information to internal and external stakeholders of the firm. The documentation of this information is internally focused on practices such as design, recycling, pollution control and waste minimization, training, reporting to top management, and the setting of goals. The use of this information for external stake-holders is primarily found in annual reports, focuses on the outputs of the firm, and is used to enhance firm image.[7] There is a growing recognition of opportunities for integrated financial and sustainability reporting. This trend of integration and transparency has caught the attention of many through recent surveys and published empirical evidence.[8]

Other notable areas of importance in the integration of sustainability include viewing this paradigm through the eyes of multiple stakeholders. One way of assessing the ability to meet objectives is to measure the extent to which sustainability is integrated and understood across all areas of a company. The use of employee surveys, stakeholder feedback, and engaging communities are all important measures of this extent of integration. With the importance of measurement, rankings, annual reports, and stakeholder engagement to understanding the extent to which organizations are sus-tainable, managers are now better able to understand this paradigm. This understanding is due to the scrutiny of sustainability in measuring and managing processes and its application into formerly uncharted territory. To take this stakeholder perspective across functions, supply chain trans-parency provides a complex and global perspective to sustainability.[9] To what extent companies can measure supply chain impacts is fundamental. The scale of this issue grows exponentially if you imagine trying to assess performance and impact of up to 25,000 suppliers to a company within the constraint of not being able to audit each supplier. Given the dynamic and complex environment of global supply chains, we need to leverage finan-cial, operational, and predictive metrics awaiting sustainability professionals when pursuing integration and collaboration in the name of sustainability.

We see sustainability professionals from leading companies have trans-lated this management paradigm into a diverse set of actionable practices. A conceptual model (Figure 3.2) of our work with MNCs highlights the primary drivers of sustainability from Volume 1, Chapters 1 and 2 while linking drivers to performance Volume 1, (Chapter 3), and the need for design and collaboration (highlighted in Volume 2, Chapter 1).

---

[7]Sroufe (2003), pp. 416–431.
[8]KPMG (2011).
[9]Accenture (2008).

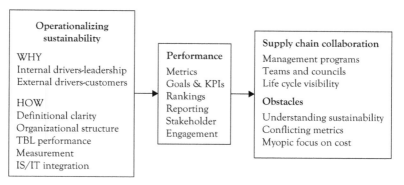

Figure 3.2 Integration of sustainability

It is worth noting management's responsibility (especially at the top) in providing clarity and attention to sustainability initiatives. Through defining and aligning sustainability with company mission and performance metrics, supply chain managers and the growing ranks of sustainability professionals will better organize teams to enable new initiatives and to better integrate social and natural capital measurement across functions. This measurement drives success with voluntary initiatives and improved performance with internal and external opportunities to report results for recognition and enhanced brand image. Compliance is not the best label for companywide integration of a voluntary paradigm; instead, a focus on "performance" and the ability to meet and exceed goals is a better approach. To ensure improved performance, supply chain and sustainability professionals must work across their organization and into their supply chains to also measure and manage the contributions of a supply chain to a company's natural capital, full life cycle impacts, social capital, and performance.

There is little doubt that both the significance and prevalence of instituting sustainability practices, within the organization overall as well as in the supply management group, is on the rise as is evident in the following.

- The 2011 MIT Sloan Management Review Research Report based on their Sustainability & Innovation Global Executive Study found that despite difficult financial times, 68 percent of organizations increased their overall sustainability commitments during the course of 2010, up from 59 percent in 2009, and only 25 percent in 2008.

- According to a series of surveys and interviews of large European corporations carried out by HEC and EcoVadis, 90 percent of supply management directors consider sustainable supply management to be an important or critical priority in 2009, versus 60 percent in 2005 and only 40 percent in 2003.
- The CDP's 2011 supply chain report, created by A.T. Kearney, found that the time period between 2009 and 2010 saw at 40 percent jump, from 46 percent to 86 percent, in the number of supply organizations who worked with their suppliers on carbon-related activities, and that 45 percent of the surveyed companies are tracking and reporting on their supply chain emissions, double those in 2009.

Supply Chain Implications for Sustainability

For the preceding findings to become viable, then managers have to recognize the need to take a more active role in developing suppliers that can support the objectives of sustainability. Specifically, this means that firms must develop and implement the following:

- An active supplier base management system.
- A system for managing system interoperability.
- A system for ensuring that we manage for more than pollution.
- A system that provides complete visibility and transparency.

Supplier Base Management

Supplier base management, as proposed by Melnyk, Griffis, Macdonald, and Phillips (2010),[10] is a proactive strategy developed by firms for developing and managing its supplier base (i.e., the upstream portion of the supply chain) so that this base is supportive of the firm's business

---

[10]Melnyk, S.A., Cooper, M.B., Griffis, S.E., Macdonald, J.R., Phillips, C.L.M. (2010). Supplier base management: a new competitive edge. *Supply Chain Management Review.* 14 (4). *pp.* 35–41.

Table 3.1 The Supplier Base—Old and New Views

Key issues	Old view	New view
Which suppliers to focus on	Current major suppliers (those that we do the most business with or who are important to our business)	Current major suppliers Minor suppliers Potential suppliers "Past" suppliers Go beyond first tier
Relationships	Current	Current AND Future
Attention spent on past suppliers	Minimal (since they are past, they are no longer important)	Great (knowledge transfer, discussion/decision on technical support)
View of the supplier base	Static (change not considered)	Dynamic (supplier base constantly changing)
How supplier base Performance is measured?	Cost Quality	Multiple dimensions including sustainability (depending on desired outcomes)
Awareness of other supply chains	Low	High

strategy and business model. Supplier base management refers to a new, emerging view of the supplier base. These differences between this new view of the supplier base and the old view are summarized in Table 3.1.

As this table suggests, the new view underlying supplier base management takes a more holistic approach. It focuses on a larger set of suppliers (current and potential), recognizes that the supplier base and supplier relationships are dynamic, and that the desired outcomes from the supplier base may include multiple competitive dimensions. Supplier-based management consists of four major activities: (a) managing the majors; (b) developing the minor suppliers; (c) scouting; and (d) transition management.

Managing the Majors: For most firms, this forms the major focal point. Major suppliers are the current set of suppliers with which the firm is working. While we assume that this set of suppliers is fixed and stable, we must recognize that these assumptions are neither appropriate nor desired. A stable supplier base at this level is attractive because we know the suppliers that we are working with. Yet, without some degree of turnover in suppliers, there is the ever-present danger that this supplier base will become complacent, generate less innovation, or be more likely to take advantage of us. Furthermore, there is also the danger that the skills present in our existing supplier base may not be consistent with our new emphasis on sustainability. In addition, a stable supplier base may not be able to respond quickly enough to changes in demand. Finally, we must recognize that suppliers can and do drop out. They do so for a number of valid reasons—bankruptcy, changes in strategic direction, or acquisition by other firms (to name a few). Consequently, we need a system for "feeding" this set of suppliers—this system is the process of minor supplier development.

Developing Minor Suppliers: Minor suppliers can be viewed as potential replacements for current major suppliers. Supplier base management fulfills a number of critical functions for the buying firm regarding its suppliers: (a) it facilitates evaluation of these suppliers by identifying capabilities, strengths, and weaknesses; (b) it allows the buying firm to shepherd these suppliers along in their development, thereby providing the buying firm a chance to encourage those good suppliers to either fill currently unmet needs, or to challenge current active suppliers for their place in the supply chain; (c) it creates an environment for supplier education, to teach the supplier about how the buying firm's system operates, how suppliers are evaluated, and the goals and core values of the buying organization; (d) it facilitates supplier integration, to smooth the process of integrating the supplier and its systems into the buying organization's system; and (e) it allows the firm to develop suppliers with capabilities different from those currently offered by major suppliers and which may be demanded in the future.

Changes in the desired outcomes (as captured in the business model) can result in the firm requiring capabilities different from those found within its current system. Critical to assessing these capabilities are the capabilities offered by its existing suppliers. That is, our capabilities are determined by both our internal factories and external factories (the suppliers). When new or changed supplier capabilities are required, managers must realize that these new capabilities may not exist in the current supply base; and that new suppliers may be needed to provide the necessary capabilities. Thus, we need to understand the difference between supplier capabilities and our own, then adjust our planning and execution systems to maximize sustainability?

Scouting: Scouting does more than simply help the firm identify potential suppliers that the buying organization can work at recruiting for itself. Scouting includes two other critical activities. First, it seeks to enhance the attractiveness of the firm as a potential partner and buyer to these desirable potential suppliers. Furthermore, scouting carries out a competitive intelligence function regarding the supply chains of major competitors. Scouting can identify potential trends, developments, and changes taking place at competitors, better positioning a firm to assess the implications of these changes. Scouting can help the firm identify what its competitors are doing with sustainability in their supply chains. Such practices and approaches may be ones that we can also use in our supply chains. More importantly, these practices and approaches may shape the expectations of our customers, when it comes to judging and understanding sustainability in our supply chain. It is ironic that while marketing encourages such activities (in the guise of marketing intelligence), such activities have received almost no notice in the supply chain management literature.

Transition Management: The last element, transition management, focuses on moving suppliers into and out of the various levels of the supplier base. The objective is to limit problems created during transition. Too often firms depend on their major suppliers for innovation, developing and maintaining drawings and material, and/or product specifications with no existing plan for transferring knowledge. When a major supplier moves out of the supplier base, the buying organization may have to address such issues as the management of intellectual property or any other knowledge that is critical to the buying organization but that resides with the supplier. Ensuring that intellectual property is protected, as well as uncovering invisible factories the buying firm may be unaware of can lead to significant challenges during supplier transition. Suppliers take with them detailed knowledge that the buying organization relies upon, knowingly or unknowingly, to ensure product quality. Exiting suppliers may not always be willing to provide this information to the buying firm or the replacement supplier, depending upon the reason for their exiting a supply chain. In other cases, departing suppliers may even hold firm assets "hostage."

A System for Managing System Interoperability

Interoperability refers to the extent to which different organizations can interface with each other. This concept exists at three levels:

- Data (can we share and use the same data).
- Processes (can we interface key processes with supply chain partners).
- Expectations (are the expectations of partners sufficiently consistent with each).

Past research has focused on the first two dimensions. Developments such as electronic data interchange (EDI) and the Supply Chain Operational Reference (SCOR) Model developed by the Supply Chain Council (http://supply-chain.org/) and discussed in Volume 1, Chapter 3 have played an important role in addressing the concerns raised by the first two levels. Consequently, this leaves us with the last form of interoperability—alignment of expectations.

The alignment of expectations is a new and increasingly critical dimension. What this dimension recognizes is that the parties entering into any relationship such as a supply chain relationship bring with them different expectations. If these expectations are sufficiently different between the parties are sufficiently different, then the relationship will not likely start.

Yet, the differences in expectations can occur in several different ways:

- We enter the relationship with different expectations and they remain different;
- We enter the relationship with different expectations and these change over time;
- We enter the relationship with similar expectations and these change over time; or,
- We enter the relationship with different expectations and they converge over time.

All of these instances, except for the last case, can create problems with any business model that is built around sustainability. The reason is that the parties may take actions that are consistent with their expectations but not with systems thinking and the expectations of the other parties involved.

To deal with these differences in expectations, firms can draw on a number of tools:

- Frequent communication, visibility, and transparency within the supply chain.
- On site visits with the aim of seeing if the actions being taken are consistent with the goals/expectations of the other party.
- Metrics and performance measurement. As pointed out in Volume 1, Chapter 3, metrics and performance measurement communicate what is important in a relationship and what is not important. It also facilitates the identification of potential problems and development of corrective actions.
- Standards that the other parties are expected to conform to it. As we have shown earlier in Volume 1, Chapter 4, these standards identify minimum levels of acceptable practices and processes that the parties are expected to implement and conform to.

By implementing these and other tools, we seek to develop a situation where the actions taken by our supply chain partners support our sustainability-based business model and they do not reflect negatively on this goal.

A System for Ensuring That We Manage for More Than Pollution

In the past, sustainability has been primarily about managing pollution. But this view is now changing. Companies now understand that sustainability is broader—it must deal with the triple bottom line. It must deal with both pollution and people. This is the lesson that we can see when we study the decisions and actions of companies such as Disney, MillerCoors, Starbucks, and Unilever.

Disney, in May 2013, announced that it would stop production of branded merchandise in five high-risk countries: Bangladesh, Ecuador, Venezuela, Belarus, and Pakistan by April 2014. The reason—these countries represented environments inconsistent with Disney's core values. These were countries that were ranked lowest by the World Bank on metrics such as accountability, corruption, and violence. In the case of Pakistan and Bangladesh, the factories there represented unsafe work environments and environments in which the workers were badly treated and poorly paid. Disney is not alone in this concern. Other companies such as J.C. Penney, Benetton, and Sears have emphatically stated their concern for worker safety and monitoring conditions. The British retailer Primark announced that it will compensate victims who worked for its suppliers—support in the form of long-term financial aid for children who lost parents, financial aid for those injured, and payments to the families of the deceased.

MillerCoors, a major American manufacturer and distributor of alcoholic beverages, has now recognized that its products can adversely affect the communities that use its products. Consequently, it is now actively working with the local communities to crack down on underage driving and to encourage and promote a designated driver program. It knows that its customers, many of whom are millennials – people born after 1977—want to consume from companies that they regard as sustainable.

Finally, Starbucks, the world's largest coffee retailer, announced on April 2015 that 99 percent of its coffee was ethically sourced. That is, the products were grown without forest canopy loss and with fair employment conditions. Over 440,000 workers on coffee farms supplying Starbucks earned better than the local minimum wage, 89 percent of the workers received sick leave, and all children living on coffee estates attended school.

As can be seen from this brief discussion, customers expect more of the sustainable supply chain than simply pollution reduction; they want supply chains that help to elevate and protect the workers that these chains employ both directly and indirectly. They want supply chains that really do make life better for everyone.

Understand that the customers now have the power to make their views and feelings known. When a company fails, consumers can react quickly by posting angry statements on Twitter or on the company's own Facebook pages. The letters to the editors have been replaced by the social media twitter.

A System That Provides Complete Visibility and Transparency

To understand this final point, consider the next generation of Supply stores—Starbucks Reserve (see https://www.youtube.com/watch?v=pBatO5_-h08). The first of these chains was opened late in 2015 in Seattle Washington—only nine blocks from the original Starbucks store. What makes this new generation so different is that it makes the coffee supply chain highly visible to the customer. When you walk into this store, you are not only greeted by the stations where coffee is brewed; you are also greeted by a fully functional coffee processing system. To the people at Starbucks, this store represents the future of Starbucks. It represents a store where the supply chain is highly visible and transparent. It is also a response to the changing demands of the consumer. As one senior Starbucks market executive put it—"Increasingly, today's consumer wants to know of the provenance of the products that they consume." That is, today's customers want to know where their products are coming from; they want—NO—demand—supply chain visibility and transparency.

This change in consumer demand is, fortunately, being met by the recent changes in technology in the form of the Internet of Things (IoT) and social media. IoT refers to the network of physical objects that are embedded with software, sensors, and network connectivity that enable the IoT to collect, communicate, exchange, and analyze data. Included in IoT are smartphones, sensors in cars and trucks, equipment, shipping containers, appliances, fitness monitors, smart watches and product tags. It is estimated that by 2020, there will be over 200 billion devices. The importance of these changes is the technology is enabling supply chain managers to track quickly and cost effectively the status and movement of products. This tracking enables and enhances the visibility and transparency of the supply chain.

Summary

In today's business environment, we must recognize the need and importance of supply chains and supply chain management. The advantages that they bring are too important to be ignored. This observation applies to sustainability. We need to incorporate the supply chain into the sustainable business model since the supply chain significantly influences the capabilities component of the business model. It offers the firm access to critical resources; it enables the firm to draw on the problem-solving and skill capabilities of its suppliers. By recognizing the supply chain, we also recognize the fact that any problems created by a supplier may become attributed to the firm (especially if these problems affect the firm's goal of competing on sustainability).

To be successful with sustainability requires that management become involved in the supply chain. This involvement takes several different forms:

- The introduction of an active supplier base management strategy.
- The alignment of expectations through frequent communication, appropriate metrics and measures, and the introduction of suitable standards.
- The firm must work to integrate the supply chain into its business model.
- The firm must focus on the broadest implementation of sustainability—a sustainable supply chain, as discussed in Volume 1, Chapter 1, incorporating financial, natural, and social forms of capital.

For any organization to be truly sustainable, it must ultimately have a sustainable supply chain.

Applied Learning: Action Items (AIs)—Steps you can take to apply the learning from this chapter

After reviewing this chapter, you should be prepared to assess internal and external supply chain integration opportunities. To aid you in this assessment, please consider the following questions:

AI: How many tiers of suppliers do you have in your supply chain, and do you know where all of your materials and components come from?

AI: What management systems are already in place that will enable sustainability as a collaborative part of how you operate your business rather than having sustainability as a peripheral activity?

AI: Does your supply chain sustainability strategy include the following dimensions:

- Labor wages relative to the average in the area?
- Working conditions within the supply chain?
- Labor treatment within the supply chain?
- Sick leave policies within the supply chain?
- Education opportunities for the children of employees within the supply chain?
- Do you rely primarily on international standards for assessing labor conditions within the supply chain or do you supplement these by other means of verification and validation?

AI: To what extent are supply chain professionals included in sustainability initiatives?

AI: What plans do you have in place to introduce IoT as a method for building supply chain visibility?

Further Readings

Bove´, A.-T., Swartz, S. (2016). Starting at the Source: Sustainability in Supply Chains. McKinsey & Company. http://www.mckinsey.com/business-functions/sustainability-and-resource-productivity/our-insights/starting-at-the-source-sustainability-in-supply-chains?cid=sustainability-eml-alt-mip-mck-oth-1611. Accessed December 3, 2016.

KPMG (2011). *Sustainability reporting-what you should know.* http://docplayer.net/236571-Sustainability-reporting-what-you-should-know-kpmg-com.html (accessed February 22, 2017).

Christensen, J., Park, C., Sun, E., Goralnick, M., Iyengar, J. (2008). A Practical Guide to Green Sourcing. *Supply Chain Management Review.* 12(8).

CHAPTER 4

Integration

Enabling People and Customers

Organizations that empower folks further down the chain or try to get rid of the big hierarchical chains and allow decision making to happen on a more local level end up being more adaptive and resilient because there are more minds involved in the problem.

—Steven Johnson

- In comparison to peers who do not actively engage employees, companies that do, can measure their competitive edge in the form of increased profitability (16 percent), improved productivity (18 percent), higher customer loyalty (12 percent) as well as decreased employee turnover (25 percent), fewer safety incidents (49 percent), and lower absenteeism (37 percent).[1]
- The annual Sustainability Executive Survey from Green Research finds 88 percent of senior sustainability executives say they plan on investing in increased employee engagement.[2]
- Since 2008, Intel has calculated every employee's annual bonus based on the firm's performance in measures such as product energy efficiency, completion of renewable energy projects, and company reputation for environmental leadership.[3] Its market share among semiconductor manufacturers has reached a ten-year high.

---

[1]Gallop (2009).
[2]Green Research (2012).
[3]Lubber (2010).

To this point, this book has emphasized what are essentially "macro" issues. That is, the focus has been on those higher level issues that involve top management committing resources and setting the overall direction of the firm. These issues involve corporate-wide investments in new tools and training. These are issues involving strategic focus. Implicit to this treatment is the assumption that the macro perspective is enough. That is, once these issues are addressed at this higher level, the rest of the organization will follow and implement the directions established at the macro level. Implicitly, with this approach, we are assuming that these other, more detailed stages have little or no impact on how an organization achieves a sustainable supply chain and that the interaction between the levels is insignificant. Ultimately, these assumptions are both spurious and highly dangerous. To be successful with sustainability, we must in the end succeed at the deployment/implementation stage. To succeed at this stage, we must in the end enable and empower the customers, the suppliers, and the employees who work within the organization; we must also empower the supply chain. Such empowerment is as important as the macro issues. It requires training, scouting, talent development, and, in some cases, significant changes in the organizational culture. Ultimately, such empowerment builds success because each and every person understands the overarching goals and their contribution to these goals. In their actions, taken every day without management overview, the people (be they customers, suppliers, or corporate employees) make the vision of sustainability into reality. How we achieve this state is the focus of this chapter.

Objectives

Building off of Chapter 3, we continue to focus on the organization of the constituent elements of individuals and processes into a coordinated, harmonious whole for the organization, and supply chain. We can also use the terms *collaboration* and *partnership* to recognize how integration is already part of commerce. Our ability to synthesize, to break complex relationships down into elemental, core requirements is essential to the integration of sustainability. The ability to look at systems and supply chains in these ways forms the core of this chapter when addressing the human element, and a roadmap to success while finding opportunities to rethink what you and your organization do on a day-to-day basis.

By the end of this chapter, you will be able to:

1. Understand the human dynamics involved in a supply chain.
2. Explore and understand how the supply chain can be used to create a viable and strong force for sustainability.
3. Apply a systematic approach, using Juran's Universal Breakthrough Sequence, to make sustainability a day-to-day habit.

Integration—The Key to the Sustainable Supply Chains

Critical to the success of the sustainability initiative, as deployed within the supply chain, is the notion of integration, or the manner in which we link the various components that make up the supply chain. *Integration* is an important term that is frequently found in discussions pertaining to the supply chain. It is also a term that is often used without any definition. Consequently, it is one of the most misunderstood terms in supply chain management.

Integration occurs at various levels: legal, processes, data, systems, information flows, and the extent to which the participants invest in each other's systems. Integration can be "tight" where the parties work together to ensure that their actions and flows are closely and continuously synchronized. Integration can also be "loose"—where the parties are bound by some set of general agreements over which they will strive to achieve when working together. Integration is important because it influences three critical supply chain traits: visibility, the ease of information flows, and the resulting relationship structure.

Visibility (previously discussed in both Volume 1 (chapter 3) and earlier in this volume) determines how far into the supply chain both upstream (through the supplies) and downstream (customers) you can effectively see. As such, visibility is important because it serves as an early warning system. That is, the greater the visibility, the earlier that the organization can identify a potential problem before it becomes serious. Visibility is akin to your ability to look down the road when driving. The farther down the road that you can see, the earlier that you can identify a change in conditions (e.g., cars slowing down) and take appropriate corrective actions. Visibility gives you the time to evaluate the situation and to consider alternative actions open to you. Without visibility, you are faced by the need to take immediate actions now, often without a lot of evaluation of the situation or the options available. Decisions made without visibility are seldom the best.

Before leaving this discussion, it is important to recognize that visibility is now becoming a corporate and business imperative. There are several reasons for this. First, there is a fundamental change taking place in the marketplace. The new customer is the millennial. These customers, typically born beginning in 1982, are different. They expect sustainability—something that firms such as MillerCoors have found; they are willing to search for such products. They will search the Internet for products that conform to their expectations. They also want to know the origin of any product that they consume. If you cannot provide such visibility, then expect to lose sales and customers.

In addition, thanks to technological advances—specifically the Internet of Things (IoT) and social media (e.g., facebook)—the ability to provide such visibility is getting easier and cheaper. We are finding ourselves living in a world of smart sensors. These sensors, found in smart phones, tags, product identifiers, and packaging, can be used to monitor location and state in real time. The IoT is providing the structure whereby visibility in real time is being created.

The second trait, ease and openness of information flow, refers to how easily and openly information and data flows between the various parties in the supply chain take place. Information flows are important since they help shape expectations and ensure that these expectations are aligned. The ease and openness of information flows contribute to the timeliness of information (i.e., early warning) and the extent to which important information is provided in advance or is made available after the fact.

The third element, relationship, focuses on the structure or governance under which the parties involved in the supply chain relationship work together. Relationships are important because they affect such supply chain traits as:

- Duration of the relationship.
- Obligations of the parties involved.
- Expectations of the parties involved.
- How the parties interact and communicate with each other.

- How planning and the setting of goals across the supply chain takes place.
- Performance measure and analysis.
- Sharing of benefits, costs, and risks.

Relationships can take many forms (transactional/arm's length versus collaboration and strategic). For the sake of simplicity, we will focus on and compare arm's length versus collaboration, as summarized in Table 4.1.

Alignment of expectations and sharing of information are easier under a collaboration relationship. But, it is also more resource intensive in that the firm has to identify the "right" partner, evaluate the partner, work on building trust and credibility, and then work on maintaining the relationship—all of which requires time, management commitment, and resources.

A second consideration is that of how tightly linked the relationships are. When we talk about tightness, we are talking about such issues as:

- Sharing of information.
- Extent to which information is "pushed" or "pulled"—that is, is information provided without being asked for (i.e., pushed) or is it provided in response to specific requests (pulled through the supply chain)?

Table 4.1 Relationships: A Comparison of Arm's Length and Collaborative

Arm's Length/transactional	Collaborative/Relationship
Short term (year or less)	Long term (often exceeding a year)
Legally defined (often by the contract)	Based on expectation of mutual benefits and trust
Limited information sharing	Extensive information sharing
Relationship viewed as a zero-sum game	Relationship viewed as a "win/win"
Relatively resource light (i.e., does not use an extensive amount of resources)	Very resource intensive
Appropriate for commodities	Appropriate for strategically important products or services

- Extent to which the information is symmetrical or asymmetrical.
- Extent to which firms make investments in each other's systems.

Relationships span a spectrum ranging from a modular system on one end to a unified system on the other. With a modular system, the firm has limited visibility into the supply chain. In most cases, this visibility can be best described as being "one up and one down"—that is, we are integrated with our immediate customers and with our immediate suppliers. Yet, beyond these, we have almost no visibility. Underlying the modular system is the implicit demand that our partners manage the problems beyond our span of attention. That is, the first-tier supplier is responsible for managing any supplier problems occurring below them; similarly, the immediate customers are required to deal with any demand-side problems. This puts a great deal of responsibility on these partners. Modular integration is relatively cost efficient. Yet, it does expose the firm to greater risks because visibility is very limited.

In contrast, there is the unified approach where relationships are being built through the various stages, with the goal of coordinating the activities. This approach gives greater visibility. With visibility, we can see beyond the first tier and identify potential problems before they can affect us. We can intervene and prevent a minor problem from becoming a major one. Yet, this visibility comes at a cost in the form of greater resources and time needed to develop this visibility. The point being raised here is that of trade-offs.

The analysis between these two competing approaches is further complicated by the increasing presence of business analytics. Business analytics is the culmination of three important trends:

- More powerful, lower-cost computers.
- More powerful software packages that are based on advanced mathematics, statistics, and other similar quantitative tools.
- Greater availability of information (also called big data).

The result is that companies such as IBM, L'Oréal, McDonalds, P&G, Unilever, and Walmart to name a few, have implemented analytics aimed at providing firms with greater visibility into their supply chains.

Supply Chain Management's Integration Opportunity

Despite ongoing attempts to integrate supply chains, many individuals and teams can be overwhelmed by the organization of data required for effective analysis to fully understand sustainability issues and opportunities. The competitive advantage a firm can derive from supply chain integration and optimization is from understanding and leveraging the emerging methods, guidelines, and standards now available to supply chain and sustainability professionals outlined in this book.

Requirements for successful supply chain management integration require communication and trust as information exchange is essential for supply chain members to understand each other, share common goals, and make decisions that are mutually beneficial. As Senge, Lichtenstein, Kaeufer, Bradbury, and Carroll, (2007) found, meeting the challenges of sustainability "writ large" would require not only supply chain integration, but also cross-sector collaboration for which there is no real precedent.[4]

Additional requirements for successful analysis require supply chain visibility leveraging information systems and data sharing with supply chain members to see into any part of a supply chain to access data on inventory levels, or the status of shipments. This visibility within supply chains is growing more expansive of both social and environmental metrics. These metrics are now included in firm performance and are solicited as part of supplier assessment programs and audits including examples such as Walmart's 2011 initiative in Table 4.2.

An important part of any analysis will be performance metrics as they are necessary to confirm whether a supply chain is functioning as planned and help identify opportunities for sustainability and performance improvement. Signaling through the Walmart supplier assessment signals the importance of energy and climate, material efficiencies, and natural resources, along with people and the community. There are a variety of traditional supply chain measures used, including but not limited to reliability, asset utilization, costs, quality, and flexibility. Performance measures and metrics involving sustainability are gaining prominence as stakeholders including supply chain customers are asking for disclosure of

---

[4]Senge et al. (2007).

Table 4.2 *Walmart's Supplier Sustainability Assessment: 15 Questions for Suppliers*[5]

Energy and climate: reducing energy costs and Green House Gases (GHG) emissions 1. Have you measured your corporate GHG emissions? 2. Have you opted to report your GHG emissions to the Carbon Disclosure Project? (CDP) 3. What is your total annual GHG emissions reported in the most recent year measured? 4. Have you set publicly available GHG gas reduction targets? If yes, what are those targets?
Material efficiency: reducing waste and enhancing quality 1. If measured, please report the total amount of solid waste generated from the facilities that produce your product(s) for Walmart for the most recent year measured. 2. Have you set publicly available solid waste reduction targets? If yes, what are those targets? 3. If measured, please report total water use from facilities that produce your product(s) for Walmart for the most recent year measured. 4. Have you set publicly available water use reduction targets? If yes, what are those targets?
Natural resources: producing high-quality, responsibly sourced raw materials 1. Have you established publicly available sustainability-purchasing guidelines for your direct suppliers that address issues such as environmental compliance, employment practices, and product/ingredient safety? 2. Have you obtained third-party certifications for any of the products that you sell to Walmart?
People and community: ensuring responsible and ethical production 1. Do you know the location of 100 percent of the facilities that produce your product(s)? 2. Before beginning a business relationship with a manufacturing facility, do you evaluate the quality of, and capacity for, production? 3. Do you have a process for managing social compliance at the manufacturing level? 4. Do you work with your supply base to resolve issues found during social compliance evaluations and also document-specific corrections and improvements? 5. Do you invest in community development activities in the markets you source from and/or operate within?

Source: Walmart Supplier Sustainability Supplier Survey, (2013). *Walmart Supplier Sustainability Assessment: 15 Questions for Suppliers*, http://az204679.vo.msecnd.net/media/documents/r_3863.pdf

social, governance, and environmental information more than any previous time in history. The pressure to measure and disclose provides a proving ground for new and innovative ways to analyze the performance of a firm or a supply chain along multiple dimensions.

---

[5]Walmart Supplier Sustainability Supplier Survey (2013).

The continued global interest in improving business management through the reduction of Greenhouse gas (GHG) is driving sustainability-focused companies and suppliers to measure and manage their carbon footprint. While environmental and social responsibility is predominately voluntary in North America, environmental mandates in regions such as the Europe have a far-reaching impact on manufacturing and logistics in the United States. The proliferation of U.S. corporate acquisitions by European and Far Eastern companies results in the sustainability policies of these parent organizations reaching around the world. In addition, suppliers of both goods and services to the leading edge sustainable organizations are beginning to see the shift from optional GHG improvement initiatives to required sustainability strategies to remain a viable supply chain partner.

Companies today are focused on shareholder and customer values, while maximizing the velocity of information transfer, reduction of waste in the system, and minimizing response time. Supply chain integration involves working across multiple enterprises or companies to remove waste, and shorten the supply chain time in the delivery of goods and services to the consumer or customer. Until recently, supply chain analysis has overlooked opportunities for systems thinking and the ability to include forward-looking strategies for firms and their supply chains involving the primary elements of sustainability, that is, the ethical management of financial, environmental, AND social capital so firms can better measure and manage supply chains with an integrated approach to performance.

Collaboration

Now, we're seeing firms such as Nestlé take the concept of "shared value" and turn it into genuine, in-depth supplier collaboration. Its work with Golden-Agri Resources on palm oil in Indonesia (a difficult operating environment to get good news stories from) could soon become a model or benchmark for supply chain transparency.

In the equally complicated and low-margin clothing industry, companies such as New Look have done amazing work with suppliers, helping them understand how to run better factories. What have better factory management practices got to do with sustainability? Everything. If you want to cut forced overtime for workers, increase productivity, reduce accidents, increase profits, and lower environmental emissions and impacts—that's all about sustainability and efficient business practices.

That's easy to say, but your average stressed shift manager or factory owner doesn't usually know how sustainable business practices can or should be applied to their workers or business operations. We must remember that most developing-country entrepreneurs and managers didn't go to business school. They didn't have much, if any, real training. They saw opportunities, and they made it up as they went along.

That makes them heroes in many ways—for taking risks, creating jobs, and lowering prices. But, the unintended consequences of that created demand have been serious impacts on the environment and human well-being, as we all know. These managers are not bad people. They just didn't understand how to do business any other way, and most still don't. Big companies must help them find out, and push them to improve. Resource efficiency, environmental impacts, and the need to hang on to workers have created a pressing business case.

We don't know of a manager or business owner anywhere who would turn down practical help to become more efficient. Making sustainability stick has to be framed in those terms. Get that right and put the resources into doing in a five-year timescale with annual reporting and measurement, and you'll be amazed at the results, for both your business, community, and the planet.

It really can be that simple. Invest in processes and practices while measuring the sustainable value added (SVA), and get a massive return on investment.

Sustainable Supply Chain Management Integration

Over the past two decades, there has been an exponentially increasing amount of published research regarding sustainability in both practitioner and academic circles. Authors in the field of supply management have increasingly come to recognize the pivotal role which the supply management professional plays in bringing to fruition an organization's sustainability vision. Yet, many organizations are overwhelmed by this information and struggle to implement basic sustainability programs.

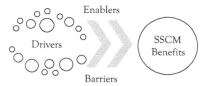

Figure 4.1 Important attributes of supply chain management integration

We turned to the literature to identify trends that both explain the current state of sustainable supply management, as well as highlight positive steps that could be taken to ease this transition.[6] We reviewed over 200 of the most pertinent articles taken from both journals and special publications. A summary of this work provides a framework illustrating the internal and external focus necessary in order to successfully achieve the significant benefits of sustainable supply management (see Figure 4.1). To realize these benefits of integrating sustainability, internal sustainability champions will have to: (a) identify and articulate the organization's drivers, (b) mitigate existing and potential barriers, and (c) embrace the enablers for this process. Within the context of these categories, we next summarize and draw lessons learned from publications spanning almost two decades.

Drivers are those actions providing motivation for sustainable supply management. The main drivers tend to be external to the organization itself, and most are reactive in nature. The most commonly cited external drivers are: (a) the reactive need for regulatory compliance, (b) proactive considerations to avoid environmental impacts, and (c) reactive replies to customer and competitive pressure.

Not surprisingly, of the drivers internal to the organization, by far the one most commonly cited is that of cost savings. However, it is interesting to note that the next three most prevalent internal drivers are pressure from employees, commitment of the founder, and championing from senior management. This points to the fact that although ideally there is alignment across the organization for the need to implement sustainable

---

[6]Nirenburg and Sroufe (2012).

sourcing management practices, it is possible to successfully approach this in either top-down or bottom-up fashion.

Barriers are typically anything that restrains or obstructs progress and barriers garnered much attention in the literature. Within this area, the most cited barriers to the implementation of sustainable supply management practices pertain to internal organizational issues including the following:

The presence of competing and incompatible corporate objectives within various supply chain participants. For sustainability to be effective, the various participants must agree that sustainability is critical. This agreement must not only be at a strategic level; but also at a cultural level. There should be a "gut" feeling among everyone in the firm that sustainability is not only strategically and economically the best option, but it is also the "right" option. In a past discussion with Dr. Robert Spekman of the Darden School of Business, the University of Virginia (and one of the research leaders into B2B relationships and collaboration), it was noted that the first and major determinant of the success of a supply chain relationship is that of similarity of corporate cultures. If you see sustainability as critical but your supplier is more interested in cost, then you will not achieve sustainability. The importance of this consistency in culture (especially when dealing with key partners) is so important that it demands that the firm visit these potential partners directly to evaluate their corporate culture and their core values (with special attention being paid to sustainability as part of the core values). As Edgar Schein[7] observed, corporate culture cannot be observed and assessed from a distance.

Incentive systems focused on short-term profits. In Volume 1, Chapter 2 of this book series, we focused on Polman and Unilever. What is interesting about Polman's approach is that he has discouraged the use of quarterly reports. The reason—focusing on such results can divert attention from sustainability to, in most cases, cost. When this occurs, we send confused messages to the rest of the organization and to the supply chain. The message that we send—sustainability is important *only as long it does*

---

[7]Schein (1993).

not negatively affect profit. This implicit message communicates to everyone that profit, not sustainability, is the key strategic motivator.

Cultural resistance to change. Corporate culture, as previously noted, is critical. In many cases, when we introduce sustainability, we are effectively introducing a significant shift in strategy. If the firm has been successful with a previous strategy (most often cost based), the corporate culture that develops over time institutionalizes the practices and approaches that made the firm successful with this prior strategies. As the corporate culture is spread through on-the-job socialization, it often creates a force for stability. Such a force is important during periods of change. However, we must recognize that culture can also act as a source of resistance when the change being introduced is both fairly significant and different. Under such conditions, to overcome the resistance offered by corporate culture requires that we must first discredit the current ways of doing things. Unless this is first done, then people will fall back to the patterns of behavior supported by the existing corporate culture. Suffice to say that discrediting the current ways of doing things (especially when the firm has been successful over the long term with these approaches) is not easy to do.

Lack of top management support. Any strategic initiative such as sustainability requires a strong message from the top that: (a) this initiative is important to the firm, (b) the initiative is one that firm is committed to, and (c) you should be prepared to support this initiative or else you leave either voluntarily (through resignation) or involuntarily (through termination). For top management support to be effective, it must be visible to everyone involved, it must be active in nature (where top management is seen as actively involved in the initiative); and it must involve both rewards and punishment. That is, the top management must be ready to reward those who work to support the implementation and attainment of the new objectives. More importantly, the top management must be seen as being prepared to act when there is credible evidence that some people (especially those people who are seen as either opinion leaders or who occupy important positions within the firm) are resisting the new initiative. As a top manager put it to one of the authors, top management must be prepared to carry out a few "public executions" (terminations that become widely known throughout the firm).

Concerns over credibility/consistency. This issue specifically refers to the supply chain. Here, we are looking at a simple issue—it is impossible to credibly ask your support chain partners to do something that you, as a corporation, are not willing to undertake. You cannot ask the supply chain to pursue sustainability initiatives and objectives when your firm is not doing so. McCormick and Company, Unilever, Steelcase, and Herman Miller can ask for sustainability from its supply chain because they themselves are leaders in their industry in pursuing and embracing sustainability internally. They have done internally first that which they then ask of their suppliers.

Supply management not having a strategic role within the organization. Finally, if the supply chain is seen as being strategically decoupled and driven by concerns of reducing price, improving quality, or ensuring on time delivery, then we cannot expect to see the supply chain embrace sustainability. To these partners, sustainability is something that will not affect them because at the end of the day, they are asked to deliver the same outcomes: price, delivery, and quality.

Other commonly cited barriers include: cost, both in terms of time and resources; an acknowledged skills and expertise gap on the part of employees; and issues around measurement and reporting such as the lack of consistent standards and the difficulty in understanding and applying consistent measures. The overarching theme from the literature indicates that sustainable supply management practices will require an organization-wide paradigm shift from established ways of doing business, and that the leaders in this area have already undertaken such a shift.

Enablers supply the means, knowledge, or opportunity for operational sustainable supply chains. This definition is consistent with the use of enablers of reverse logistics;[8] supply chain performance measurement system implementation,[9] and current research in sustainable supply chains.[10] This area of sustainable supply management practices has received the most attention over the years. Important internal enablers for you and your management team to focus on starts with (a) linking

---

[8]Ravi and Shankar (2005).

[9]Charan et al. (2008).

[10]Grzybowska (2012), Chapter 2.

sustainability to overall organizational strategy, (b) making supply management a strategic activity within the organization, (c) gaining and maintaining top management support, and (d) adopting a proactive approach together with a long-term perspective toward both the business itself as well as to issues of sustainability.

Important external enablers include opportunities to increase the following to support any sustainability initiative: cooperative, trusting, and transparent communication with suppliers; establishing effective supplier evaluation systems that include both rewards and penalties; using cross-functional teams for collaboration in the areas of innovation and process improvement; and increasing cross-functional education in the area of sustainability.

What are the Benefits of Sustainable Supply Chain Management?

Paradoxically, the benefits of sustainable supply chain management (SSCM) form the fundamental reason for undertaking the sustainability challenge. It is not surprising that in this area both direct and indirect financial benefits garner attention. Overall, the most commonly found benefits include: (a) a reduction of costs, including a product's whole life costs and the organization's overall operating costs; (b) increased competitive advantage and differentiation; (c) increased profits; (d) decreased damage to the environment and human health, (e) increased levels of innovation, (f) the potential to gain new customer market segments, and (g) risk mitigation.

Transforming supplier business models is the corporate strategy of the future. Because much of your firm's impacts are likely to be in your supply chain (there are exceptions), it makes sense to integrate the chain as early as possible. Today, lots of large companies, including 85 percent of the global 250, have or are developing sustainability reports with specific goals and targets. Many even have holistic "plans" with ambitious 2020 and 2050 targets across their business. But for many businesses, making these plans happen and making them have an impact internationally are going to be about sustainable change in how suppliers operate.

Companies that lead the way on sustainability have been pioneering longer-term and more in-depth supplier relationships for years. For them, this is not new. These companies include Nike (technical training for suppliers), Unilever (smallholder farmers), Marks & Spencer (eco factories), and Sainsbury's (bananas). Cadbury, before being acquired by Kraft, was also developing long-term supplier partnerships with cocoa-producing villages in Ghana. One long-standing approach to sustainability and closing the loop on supplier relations involves the concept of reverse logistics.

Reverse Logistics—Managing Returns of Material through the Supply Chain

For most firms, their responsibility to a product or service is largely defined by their position of title. Title legally defines ownership—when you have title to something, you own that entity. Physical possession is not enough to define ownership (e.g., shoplifting is possession without title and is considered a crime). Responsibility is that state where we are liable to answer for how we manage an asset or activity. In the past, the possession of title was seen as defining ownership. When you had title to a product, you were responsible; when you sold something, you were no longer responsible for it. Today, with sustainability, that is no longer the case.

Firms are now realizing that their responsibility is present in nearly all stages of the product life cycle. However, increasingly managers are looking to the end of product life stage as an opportunity for improving sustainability and fully integrate closed-loop supply chains and a circular economy. Firms are now realizing that by taking better control of returns and products that are being disposed, they can gain certain major advantages, namely,

- Opportunity to learn why products are returned or why they reach the end of their lives. When a product is thrown away or incorrectly returned, the firm has no opportunity to uncover why the product was returned or thrown away. Such information could positively influence product design and quality.
- Opportunity to return useful products back to the market. Customers return products for a number of reasons. By taking control of these products, firms can evaluate them to identify the reasons

for the returns. For those products that are still useable, these items can be returned at a discount to the marketplace. For those products that are in need of repair, these can be repaired and returned. In other cases, the products or the components contained within them can be remanufactured and sold/used for other uses such as repairs.

- Opportunity to properly dispose of waste and sensitive material. For those products that must be disposed of, the firm can ensure proper disposal. During this stage, the firm can potentially recycle the raw materials or it can ensure that, if there are any potentially damaging items (i.e., hazardous materials or sensitive data), they are appropriately dealt with. Consequently, the firm can reduce its exposure to end-of-life risks.

- Opportunities to recycle products and/or their components. McDonald's UK has been able to improve its performance by using the same trucks that delivered products to its stores to collect cardboard for recycling. This approach is not unique to McDonald's. Companies such as Shaw, Mohawk, and Monsanto are now making carpets from recycled materials. In many cases, old carpets are being converted into new carpets. By capturing these returns, firms are able to prevent these old products from being thrown away in landfills. Product take back and recycling have also been embraced by the electronics industry and by such companies as Acer, Apple, Cisco, Dell, Hewlett-Packard, Lenovo, Mitsubishi, Panasonic, Philips, Samsung, Sharp, Sony, Toshiba, and Vizio. This initiative has also been embraced by retailers such as Best Buy and Target.

These and other considerations have driven firms to consider such initiatives as reverse logistics.

. . . the process of planning, implementing, and controlling the efficient, cost effective flow of raw materials, in-process inventory, finished goods and related information from the point of consumption to the point of origin for the purpose of recapturing value or proper disposal. More precisely, reverse logistics is the process of moving goods from their typical final destination for the purpose of capturing value, or proper disposal. Remanufacturing and refurbishing activities also may be included in the definition of reverse logistics.[11]

The successful implementation of such initiatives requires the active involvement of the supply chain. In some cases, the firm can outsource the recovery activities to other firms that are experts in this area. In other cases, the firm must depend on the stores to help in the returns and must work with its supplier to ensure proper disposal of the returned product.

Putting Sustainability into Practice

We know business sustainability works best when cross-functional teams and entire supply chains are involved and enabled. Sustainability is here to stay, and the supply management group is a significant player in any organization's success in this arena. Based on our review of published research and our own insight from working with companies integrating sustainability, we recommend that you take the following steps in order to reap the benefits of sustainability-based supply management:

1. Identify and engage your internal champions of sustainability at whatever level of the organization they may be.
2. Conduct a self-audit to identify the primary drives in support of sustainability initiatives within your organization.
3. Scrutinize and create a plan to mitigate or overcome the barriers you will encounter.
4. Research, operationalize, and maximize the available enablers while recognizing the need for employee engagement.

Employee Engagement

We have always measured processes and practices, but we still do not fully understand metrics and engagement. Juran and others over time have repeatedly told us that the greater the level of detail we go to for in a process, the better we understand and can manage for efficiency and

---

[11]Hawks (2006).

effectiveness. To this end, many companies are changing internal practices to align with sustainability.

Intel has been pushed by investors for years to address issues of say-on-pay, the human right to water, and sustainability as part of a board's fiduciary obligation. So, it's not surprising that Intel links employee compensation to sustainability results. What is surprising is that Intel is doing this *for its entire workforce*. Since 2008, every single employee's annual bonus is calculated on the basis of the firm's performance on measures like product energy efficiency, completion of renewable energy and clean energy projects, and the company's reputation for environmental leadership. Last year, Intel added into the equation performance on reducing the company's carbon footprint. This is a smart move that will empower employees up and down the organization to find reductions big and small.

National Grid is an energy management and delivery company focusing on meeting the needs of customers in Massachusetts, New York, and Rhode Island. Its compensation model shows how to embed sustainability practices into a company's DNA. In talking with company president Tom King recently, we asked how he knows that sustainability is really being addressed in his company. His instant response was that it's part of everyday conversation at National Grid, and that there are no executive meetings that don't touch on environmental performance. Like Intel, National Grid has tied CEO and other executive compensation to performance on the company's GHG reduction goals. But, what's most interesting here is how aggressive those goals are: an 80 percent reduction by 2050, with 45 percent by 2020. That's a lot of executive pay at stake—and this from a major electric power utility.

All of these examples help to highlight the level of detail necessary to understand processes and the importance of engagement. To next look at a roadmap for understanding a proven approach to problem solving, we again turn to Juran and one of his well-known processes.

A Proven Approach to Integrating Problem Solving

Juran is well known for developing a systematic approach to total quality management (TQM). His goal, in developing this approach, was to make quality into a habit. For quality to become a habit, it had to be the result of a repeatable process. This process was termed the Universal Breakthrough Sequence (UBS). This logic applies equally well to sustainability as a focal point as it applies to the proven benefits of TQM.

The very first step in this process is the **creation of an awareness of need for a change.** Without this awareness, people and organizations would not change. After all, a person changes when faced with compelling evidence that the current ways of doing things were no longer succeeding. The way to create this awareness is through a self-audit (Figure 4.2). Such a self-audit helps show the participant where they are doing a good job and those areas in which they are encountering problems. It enables the participant to answer a simple but critical question: Is our system (or are our current practices) adequate to help the organization achieve its desired outcomes (and, if not, where are the changes most needed)?

Without such an audit, no change is possible because you have not shown the person or the organization that the current systems or practices are no longer sufficient. Consequently, no change will take place because no compelling reason for change has been provided.

Juran defines breakthrough as "the organized creation of beneficial change" and has observed that all breakthrough follows a universal pattern:

Proof of the need: Draw attention to the "heavy losses" incurred by companies not effectively managing the systems they are charged with leading. Show the "dangers of managing by visible figures alone" and that "the most important figures for management are the unknown and unknowable." Sustainability remains so elusive to many managers that this "unknown" performance opportunity may be the key to unlock the performance measurement revolution. The question sustainability invokes is how to draw manager's attention to a sustainability project when they are so busy living with "business as usual" that they have learned to endure the levels of chronic waste? Juran suggests using quick estimating approaches to assess the costs of waste with the aim to "bring chronic troubles out of their hiding places and convert them to alarm signals."

Yet, central to this overall sequence is proof of need. **Critical to audits are metrics.** Metrics are not simply used for control; they also facilitate communication. When we measure something, we strongly indicate to everyone that what we are measuring is important; conversely, the act of

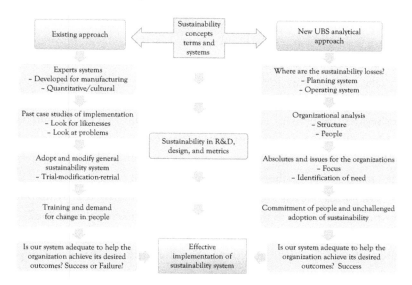

Figure 4.2 Modified UBS approach to make sustainability a habit

not measuring something indicates that the issue is not important (purposeful communication). Metrics facilitate communication between four stakeholders:

1. Top management
2. Subordinates
3. Customers
4. Suppliers

   Project identification: Use Pareto principles to find the sustainability opportunities that will have the greatest impact. Separate the vital few projects from the useful many. To help do this, understand the differences between symptoms of problems and finding underlying problems. The vital few are interdepartmental and can have multifirm performance metrics that become the responsibility of management. A starting place for where to find opportunities comes from the key metrics outlined earlier in this chapter within the section on the rise and current state of SSCM (energy efficiency, GHG emissions, water consumption, solid waste, product attributes, environmental exposure, benchmarking sustainability indices, and indexing carbon to products and revenue) as these metrics and associated projects are already used by successful multinational companies recognized as leaders in sustainable practices.

Organization to guide each project: Establish a sustainability team to take responsibility for nominating projects, assigning teams, providing resources, assessment of progress, dissemination of results, and to revise merit systems to include sustainability improvement. Simultaneously, upper management must serve on the team, approve strategic goals, allocate resources, review progress, give recognition, serve on some project teams, and revise the merit system accordingly.

Diagnosis—breakthrough in knowledge: For analysis of symptoms, formulate theories as to the causes of the symptoms, test the theories.

Remedial action on the findings: When seeking remedies, choose alternatives, take remedial actions, then deal with resistance to change, and then establish controls to hold the gains. New metrics should be the basis of a business case for a project, align with the business model, and include sustainability. Metrics consist of measures, standards, and consequences. Metrics can be measures at the end of a process. The measure represents the numbers, while the overall metric provides an opportunity for understanding and managing which leads to auditable consequences. Metrics become the basis for constructing a business case around a program or process and, when we drill down deep enough, become the basis for providing a business case behind an initiative. Keep in mind, in a world of no mirrors and no scales; we are all thin and beautiful. We need metrics to help us manage and make decisions that align with our chosen business model and integrated sustainability initiatives.

Breakthrough in cultural resistance: Getting people to change deeply held beliefs is difficult. Take for example Juran, who uses the story of the Earth-centered believers of the 14th century. The believers rejected the logical argument of the astronomers that the Earth revolved around the Sun, partly because they could see the Sun revolving around the Earth. The idea that the Earth was the center of the Universe had come down from revered religious teachers. In the light of such evidence the old beliefs could not be rejected—it was easier to burn the astronomers! Juran recommends providing participation, starting small, providing enough time, work with the recognized leadership, and dealing directly with the resistance.

Control at the new level: Continuously improve, change, and adapt to new opportunities through understanding systems and the interconnected process linking supply chains and value chains.

Paradoxically simple, yet deeply difficult, this approach to continuous improvement and the integration of sustainability into supply chain management provides a roadmap for any new program rollout or project.

Never tell people how to do things. Tell them what to do and they will surprise you with their ingenuity.
—General George Smith Patton, Jr.

Summary

The people and customers up and down a supply chain impact the success of new initiatives. Understanding relationships and the need to collaborate for success underscores SSCM opportunities. For those already integrating sustainability and supply chain partners there are known benefits of cost reduction, operational benefits, competitive advantage, decreased damage to the environment and human health, and increased innovation to name a few. Transforming supplier business models and supply chains is the corporate strategy of the future.

To be successful with sustainability requires that management become involved in supply chain management. This involvement can take several different forms:

- Collaboration.
- Assessment.
- Reverse logistics and circular economies.
- Employee engagement.
- Use of proven approaches such as the UBS.

For any organization to receive the full benefits of sustainability, it must have an integrated approach to SSCM.

Applied Learning: Action Items (AIs)—Steps you can take to apply the learning from this chapter

After reviewing this chapter, you should be prepared to assess internal and external supply chain integration opportunities. To aid you in this assessment, please consider the following questions:

AI: What kind of relationships do you have with members of your supply chain?

AI: How would the UBS help integrate sustainability into your operations and supply chain?

AI: How will you know when you have a sustainable supply chain?

AI: What is your perception of the amount of integration within your existing supply chain?

AI: In what ways have customers asked your organization for social or environmental information within request for quotation (RFQ) or request for proposals (RFPs)?

Further Readings

Elkington, J., & Branson, R. (2014). The Breakthrough Challenge: 10 Ways to Connect Today's Profits with Tomorrow's Bottom Line, Jossey-Bass.

Mohin, T. (2012). *Changing business from the Inside out*. Sheffield, UK: Greenleaf Press.

Senge, P.M., Lichtenstein, B., Kaeufer, K., Bradbury, H., Carroll, J.S. (2007). Collaborating for systemic change. *Sloan Management Review*. 48(2): 44–53.

Stringer, L. (2009). *The green workplace-sustainable strategies that benefit employees, the environment, and the bottom line*. New York, NY: Palgrave Macmillan.

Sustainable Supply Chain Management—Planning and Future Systems

CHAPTER 5

Sustainable Systems—Order Winners of the Future

More and more companies are extending their commitment to be responsible business practices to their value chains, from subsidiaries to suppliers. They do so not only because of the inherent social and environmental risks and the governance challenges the supply chain poses, but also because of the many rewards supply chain sustainability can deliver.

—George Kell, Executive Director of the United Nations Global Compact

- A study by Johnson Controls found that 96 percent of Generation Y respondents are highly concerned about the environment and expect that employers will take steps toward becoming more sustainable. Over 70 percent of respondents want business to make a real commitment to sustainability.[1]
- Ford Motor Company hires climate scientists to be part of their planning process and integration of sustainability into decision making. Setting a scenario limit on carbon emissions at 450 parts per million (ppm), Fords' management makes product development and supply chain decisions while considering future scenario planning and this self-imposed limit.

---

[1]Stika (2010).

- The new U.S. workforce increasingly comprises individuals who seek the opportunity to make a contribution to society, and who are choosing jobs that enable them to make this a part of their lives. Case in point, 92 percent of millennials say they want to work for environmentally conscious firms,[2] and over 90 percent of millennials say that a company's success should be measured by more than profit, and over 50 percent say they think businesses will have a greater impact than any other societal segment—including government—on solving the world's biggest challenges.[3]

The vignettes we use at the start of each chapter highlight leading companies involved in sustainable supply chain management (SSCM), risks of not being prepared for this business paradigm, and already apparent trends. The examples used in this chapter highlight a number of important facts motivating the need for any organization to cross the chasm and implement the concepts and practices outlined in this book. Why? Because your employees want to be involved in sustainable business practices, leading firms are already integrating sustainability into risk management and even hiring climate scientists so they can be part of teams involved in strategic planning activities, and while we implicitly allow existing systems to be wasteful we now recognize greenhouse gas (GHG) emissions and carbon as a measure of this waste knowing that it has a monetary value. Finally, we will need both an internal and external approach to engaging stakeholders for the successful implementation of SSCM.

The overarching goal of this book is to help you better understand SSCM. In doing so, we want you to see your own organization through the lens of sustainability, find intersection opportunities, leverage existing management systems, and evaluate new ways to create value for your organization and supply chain. In this chapter, we take an integrative and forward-looking approach to SSCM with the following objectives.

---

[2]Mohin (2011).
[3]Deloitte (2011).

Objectives

1. Utilize evidence-based management examples of companies successfully developing sustainable supply chains to drive value.
2. Provide a structured approach to planning and implementation.
3. Review the self-assessment process.

Ford Motor Company

We have asked managers within different industries to relate a story of how their firm changed its strategy using sustainability to guide that change process. While many firms understand the importance of planning for the future we next want to highlight one of them. According to the management at Ford, one of the big enablers of product strategy transformation from a sustainability standpoint was CO_2 emissions. If you look at the carbon footprint of Ford, you have the effects created by the vehicles they produce and customers use, manufacturing facilities, suppliers' facilities, and dealerships. When reviewing the firm's carbon footprint, and these elements up and down the supply chain, you find that 98 percent of Ford's footprint comes from their products in use. Thus, the biggest impact Ford can have is to increase fuel economy and, as a result, reduce GHG emissions.

A turning point for Ford was found in the 2007 International Panelon Climate Change (IPCC) report on the impact of climate change, temperature increases, and the tracking of ppm of CO_2. Using this report as a catalyst, the leadership at Ford now have climate scientists employed within the company and has publicly acknowledged climate change is real. These scientists have come up with an internal glide path targeting a global 450 ppm threshold. While the targeted number of 450 is debatable as being too high, the fact that CO_2 and science are shaping design and strategy decisions is not. The algorithm used helps management to understand their global CO_2 targets for any year in the future. You can name the year and management can tell you what their CO_2 targets are, and their business unit's share of allowable CO_2. Ford's decision makers are enamored with this because it provides them with a stable set of guidelines per year that do not change. This way, they know what their fleet and product development should look like one year from now, five years from now, or ten years from now. How did this come about? Starting in

2007 and 2008, Ford's management teams actually went out and worked with environmental groups such as the Union of Concerned Scientists, Environmental Defense Fund, and others. What they gleaned from these stakeholders is that the most important thing is to get started with an approach to sustainability indicatives based on data and performance metrics such as CO_2.

Why is CO_2 so important? First, it is an indication of waste as was reviewed in Volume 1, Chapters 2 and 3. Second, consider that China has seven carbon trading platforms. This recognition of emissions as having a price associated with them is substantial given China is the manufacturer to the world and has been the largest emitter of CO_2 in absolute terms for the past few years. Simultaneously, California has launched a carbon trading platform where prices are around $15 a ton. Carbon may be the first environmental waste to have a price in most of the major economies of the world, and CO_2 certainly will not be the last. Carbon markets are now planned for or operating in Europe, Korea, and Australia where prices are around $23 a ton, and the United States can point to the California exchange as its current model of success. Consequences of measuring GHG emissions with a focus on CO_2 include driving manufacturing back into countries where it was previously outsourced and the development of

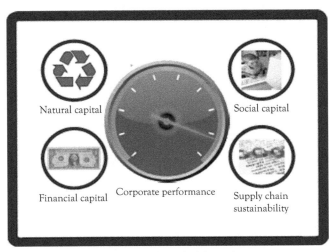

Sustainability dashboard

Figure 5.1 Dashboards of the future

distributed manufacturing systems within countries to minimize supply chain distances traveled simultaneously lowering GHG emissions.

Introduction

Motivation for the information presented in this book is a call for a better understanding of SSCM and the successful implementation of new programs. As defined early in Volume 1, SSCM is the integration of systems thinking and action into supply chain management that must include financial, AND environmental, AND social performance. These SSCM practices include stakeholder engagement, materiality, product/process design, life cycle assessment (LCA), materials selection and sourcing, manufacturing processes, waste, transportation of final products and services to consumers as well as end-of-life management of products and closed-loop systems. Systems thinking brings with it a more comprehensive approach to analysis that focuses on the way that a system's constituent parts interrelate and how systems work over time.[4] This definition of SSCM is positioned within the context of business models, frameworks, and tools for selecting and developing operations and supply chain management practices. While supply chain management calls for assessing and using information to make long-term decisions regarding supply chain strategy, having a strategy is not enough. Key to any successful strategy is the need to integrate suppliers and important metrics into processes management. Information in this chapter deals with how firms should implement SSCM. To integrate this paradigm into the long-term planning processes of a firm, we will next address implementation practices (see Figure 5.2) such as self-assessment, education, integration, vision, and communication, as they are all important for developing and delivering a SSCM strategy.

The Future of SSCM

Before addressing what we see as the future of the sustainable supply chain, it is important that we return to the discussion of the various types

---

[4]Meadows (2008).

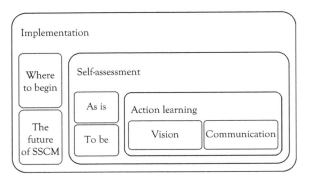

Figure 5.2 Planning and implementation architecture

of sustainability strategies introduced in Volume 1, Chapter 2. In this discussion, we pointed out that sustainability can be implemented in one of three major forms:

- Sustainability as Public Relations: This is an opportunistic approach—one in which the firm is not really committed to sustainability. Rather, it looks to any actions that it takes and sees if there is sustainability "angle" that can be publicized. Simply put, this is spin management with a sustainability perspective.
- Sustainability as Cost Minimization: With this approach, management focuses on the waste aspects of sustainability. Pollution, one of the major undesired outputs found in systems that are not sustainable, can be regarded as a form of waste. Waste adds significantly more to costs than it does to revenue. Consequently, drawing on the various tools and procedures offered by Lean, the firm strives to reduce waste and ultimately cost by focusing on sustainability. While very attractive in the short term, we must ultimately recognize that the long-term attractiveness of this approach is limited. Diminishing marginal returns plays a role. Over time, we find ourselves spending more and more time, efforts, and resources on smaller and smaller returns.
- Sustainability as Value Maximization: Here, we see sustainability as linked to the firm's strategy and as an integral element of its business model. With this approach, the firm is committed to

sustainability because it enables the firm to offer more value to its key customers, The result is often higher revenues, not simply lower costs. Higher revenues, associated with market growth, are very attractive pulls for upper management.

As we move into the future, the first critical finding is that "sustainability as Public Relations" will become less viable. This prediction has a very high probability of taking place. First of all, customers are becoming far more knowledgeable, educated, and critical when it comes to sustainability. Smart phone apps such as GoodGuide (goodguide.com), or websites such as sourcemap.com provide a wealth of transparency and visibility like never before. They can look up companies and their activities and can read what others have written about these companies. Unless they see a viable, well-thought out strategy underlying the sustainability announcements, customers are likely to dismiss these claims.

This factor was recently driven home to one of the authors, who were asked to do a sustainability presentation for a major company located in the Midwest. In preparing for this presentation, the author decided to select certain companies that he viewed as exemplar in terms of sustainability reporting. One of the firms selected was Unilever; the other was an internationally known manufacturer and distributor of consumer beverages. In presenting the various reports generated by this latter company, the author was challenged by one of the participants. The participant remarked that the statistics and the presentations provided by this company were really defensive in nature. After all, the participant argued, this company was primarily selling sugared water, which was adversely affecting health worldwide. The reports did not address this problem; rather, they seemed to argue that any adverse health issues should be weighed in terms of the other benefits that this company was creating. To this participant, this was simply window dressing and it should be dismissed. What was interesting was that this position was shared with other participants. To these participants, what they saw was sustainability as public relations and they rejected this position.

The second factor is that of the "CNN effect." The CNN effect is a notion that is frequently heard by researchers and writers working in the humanitarian/disaster relief area. What this means is that in today's world, the media is no longer willing to accept any claims made by firms.

Rather, every claim will be investigated and, if found to be false or unsupported, the negative results will be communicated quickly through print, television, on the radio and over the Internet. In other words, when a firm screws up on sustainability, it is immediately evident to the rest of the world thanks to a demanding and intelligent press/media. Apple has experienced this effect first hand as have other companies such as Nike and the Body Shop.

The third factor is the changing nature of the consumer basis. Increasingly, the major consumer driving force of the past, the baby boomers, are dying out (both literally and figuratively) and they are being replaced by the millennials. The common definition of a millennial is any person born between 1982 and 2002. These consumers began arriving into the marketplace in 2003. What companies are quickly finding is that these consumers see things differently as compared to the baby boomers.

Specifically, these consumers brought with them a new set of attitudes. It was not enough to offer these buyers a good product. What these consumers wanted were products to be responsibly produced. Furthermore, they have a very broad view of sustainability—one that goes beyond pollution. They are concerned about whether the companies they buy from offer real opportunities for advancement and promotion in the management for women and minorities. They are also technologically savvy—they can use vehicles as the Internet and social media to track and evaluate how companies are actually performing. If a company is found to be deficient, then this finding can be quickly dispersed to other interested millennials. Since this market was the growth segment, these issues have to be addressed with real action.

The second critical finding is that we can expect to see sustainability and SSCM as continuing to expand and drive business value. That is, we expect to see more and more firms integrating sustainability into their business strategies and, more importantly, into their business models. Why? There are several reasons for this shift. First, firms such as Ford, IBM, Unilever, Walmart, and other innovators and Early Adopters have already provided the proving grounds for proof of more efficient and effective value creation. For a synopsis of studies showing the business case for sustainability see "Sustainability Pays," a project by Natural

Capitalism Solutions.[5] Consequently, the risks of being a first mover (i.e., moving first and picking a development that ultimately does not succeed, e.g., picking Betamax over VHS in the tape wars) have been significantly reduced by the efforts of these companies. Second, customers are now increasingly expecting sustainability as part of the value proposition. Third, if we want to maintain our competitive positions in the marketplace, we are now expected to respond by matching the major sustainability-based moves initiated by our competition.

In addition, the various forces impacting SSCM are long term, persistent, and significant. These forces are due to resources (resource scarcity and increased competition), customer demand, government (especially in the developing countries—as many want what they see in North America and Europe), and transparency. Regarding this last dimension—transparency—consider the impact of technology. Increasingly, we now recognize that we are living in a world of smart devices (smartphones, sensors in cars, smart watches, and products). These smart devices are now collectively referred to as the *Internet of Things* (IoT). It is now estimated that there will be over 200 billion smart devices by 2020. IoT is making the development of true supply chain visibility both feasible and cost effective. The combination of these factors is changing the playing field for sustainability.

In the current and future business environments, sustainability must be seriously considered. When effectively used, it can become an order winner; when poorly deployed or overlooked, it will be an order loser.

Will everyone become sustainable? The answer is no! In reflecting on this question we return to the importance of systems design and the Crossing the Chasm model. Some firms are Innovators and Early Adopters while others are Laggards; yet the majority of organizations fall somewhere in between. Some have already said that sustainability has neared a tipping point.[6] How we will respond to the sustainability challenge depends on the type of managers we are and the type of firms in which we operate. A key aspect of this is organizational culture and the ability of management to implement new business paradigms.

---

[5]Natural Capitalism Solutions (2012).
[6]MIT Sloan Management Review and Boston Consulting Group (2012).

Will I succeed? Not necessarily! But by understanding current processes and trying at least, you increase your chance for success. Remember—not trying = 0 chance for success. The information outlined in this book provides guidelines, frameworks, performance metrics, and standards that increase the probability of a successful outcome. Sure, you can take a narrowly focused approach to SSCM, define it, and maybe do just enough to be able to market some of your actions. To do so comes with a reality check from the point of view of your competition and stakeholders. Deming's admonition, made for TQM, equally applies to the SSCM. He was once approached by a CEO who asked if he, the CEO, had to do everything that Deming had identified as being important and necessary. "No," Deming replied. "You don't have to do everything. Survival, after all, is not mandatory."

Planning and Implementation

If we are to be successful with sustainability, it must become part of our day-to-day life, business model, our core values, and those of our supply chain. It must become part of our strategy and our corporate culture. This is a major challenge and it is one that we must recognize. Although strategic planning is entrenched deeply in the minds of corporate managers and market planners, SSCM will need to be diffused throughout the organization and across functions. Before SSCM can truly affect long-range decisions at the corporate level, decision makers must first understand, develop, and implement strategic planning more effectively at the department level. The corporate planning process must incorporate more effective, integrative, and coordinating mechanisms among the various components of the strategic planning process. The end result must ultimately enhance a firm's ability to create value.

Any manager typically can see only part of the picture when looking at a supply chain. A few decades ago, researchers found purchasing personnel, especially at higher levels, do not spend a sufficient amount of time and energy on such important strategic activities as external monitoring.[7] Unfortunately, this is still true in some late adopting and Laggard

---

[7]Spekman and Hill (1980).

firms today. Unless high-level personnel concentrate to a greater degree on these external relationships they will not be able to have a positive impact on a firm's strategic planning process.

We are now more aware of the social/cultural side of change and of the organization. What we have yet to address is the issue of culture and implementation. Through decades of empirical research, researchers have established numerous relationships between organizational culture and performance. Organizational cultures (i.e., collaborative, competitive, creative, and controlling to name a few) will have different approaches to structure their solutions and thus account for the important role that culture plays in the planning and implementation of new initiatives. Next, we will use action learning as one applied approach to tackling the implementation process.

Action Learning

There is a growing need to unlock the capacity for all personnel to contribute to problem solving. One means of identifying and integrating sustainable supply chain practices is through action learning. This applied approach to problem solving and learning is defined as "a personal and organizational developmental approach applied in a team setting that seeks to generate learning from human interaction arising from engagement in the solution of real-time (not simulated) work problems."[8] We know from previous chapters that teams are important to the success of any initiative, yet we all have the same question at the beginning of a new initiative.

How do you begin this journey? First, begin by understanding why you want to become sustainable. Do not blindly jump into SSCM thinking everyone will understand or see this opportunity the same way you do. It has taken over forty years for the environmental movement to get to where it is today. Your efforts should be purposeful and focused. Understand what you want out of sustainability and why you are pursuing this initiative (e.g., efficiency, waste reduction, revenue, risk reduction, flexibility, brand image).

Second, create a compelling argument for change. Understand that people in your organization are being asked to undertake change almost

---

[8]Raelin (2006), pp. 152–156.

every day. They have been asked to undertake the TQM journey, implement Lean Systems, become more innovative, and to transform their business relationships from being transactional to being collaborative. Your call for sustainability is simply another demand being added to the pile of demands. This situation is not simply good or bad; it is simply business reality. Because countless demands have failed in the past or have been replaced by the new "management revolution of the month," many organizational members have adopted a very simple but effective approach—nod your head as if you understand, listen politely, and then keep doing what you are currently doing that works.

If we are to overcome this management inertia, we must first build a compelling business case. There are two aspects to this business case that must be emphasized. The first and one that most people focus on is to provide a quantitative assessment of costs and benefits that demonstrates the significant advantage offered by sustainability. Yet, you have to do the second part—to demonstrate to the participants that what is currently being done no longer works. We have to effectively discredit the current practices. Unless we do this, people will simply return to what they used in the past. Better the devil that you know rather than the devil that you don't know.

In developing this business case, education and understanding will be key to this undertaking. Start with an understanding of the "As Is" state of your current operations and supply chain practices. Apply known process-mapping approaches, standards, and make sure you have the necessary tools as outlined in Volume 1, Chapters 4. Secure top management support and make sure you have the time, resources, and commitment necessary. An audit of current practices and self-assessment will be just the start of the implementation process. With an understanding of current operations and supply chain practices, you can then start making decisions regarding how you will lead your given organization on the implementation of SSCM based on evidence and opportunity identification.

Assessment at the Macro and Corporate Levels

This book argues that the stage has been set for the extension of environmental management to SSCM within many original equipment manufacturers and transportation providers already driving new forms of business value. Have we gone far enough? The answer, not yet. To truly begin addressing this challenge, we need to assess events and performance at both the macro level (fit with strategy level) and the micro (performance within the firm level) level.

Self-assessment at the Strategic Level

One way to assess how far we have to go would be Hart's Sustainability Portfolio tool found within the Harvard Business Review article, "Beyond Greening" can provide insight as to how far we still need to go to reach tomorrow's potential (Figure 5.3). This tool can help you determine whether your current strategy is consistent with sustainability. This process involves a macro level self-assessment AND rating of your organization's capability in each of the four quadrants by answering the questions within each. Modern portfolio theory would suggest business managers can construct this portfolio to maximize expected returns given the level of risk and Hart suggests a balanced approach to maximizing returns.

- Many organizations will find themselves primarily in the lower left quadrant, with an emphasis on pollution prevention. Without

	Internal	External
Tomorrow	**Clean technology** Is the sustainability of our products limited by our existing core capabilities? Is there potential to realize major improvements through new disruptive technology?	**Sustainability vision** Does our corporate vision direct us toward the solution of social and environmental problems? Does our vision guide the development of new technologies, markets, products, and processes for new critical customers?
Today	**Pollution prevention** Where are the most significant waste and emission streams from our current operations? Can we lower cost and risk by eliminating waste at the source or by using it as a useful input?	**Product stewardship** What are the implications for product design and development if we assume responsibility for a product's entire life cycle? Can we change our value proposition (add value or lower costs) while simultaneously reducing the impact of our products?

Figure 5.3 The sustainability portfolio

Source: Adopted from Hart (1997).

investments in new technologies, core capabilities, and new markets, the company's environmental strategy will be vulnerable to market forces in the future.

- A portfolio with high scores in the top half can be construed as a vision without the capabilities to implement it. Internal strengths are indicative of innovation, while external strengths are aligned for anticipating new markets and sustainable development.
- A portfolio with higher scores in the left half represents an ability to address environmental issues through internal process efficiency and new technology. A focus on today is efficient but will miss out on the innovation of tomorrow.
- A portfolio with higher scores in the right half can overlook facility-level operations, core capabilities, and technology as operations will be causing more environmental and social impact than is necessary. A focus on today can be construed as a right to operate aligned with industrial ecology.

Hart's macro level assessment is a good place to start when wanting to understand the larger picture and potential vision of SSCM.

There is now a new opportunity to look at the primary enablers of a value chain, this being the transportation industry's financial, AND environmental, AND social value maximization. Why the transportation industry? New evidence has shown that over 80 percent of this economic sector's ecological footprint is captured within direct carbon emissions and purchased energy inputs.[9] With new information now available to them, firms across industries are starting to research the life cycle implications of their products and services that include transportation, and the use of products. Decision makers in those sectors should also think about the implications of measuring and managing their supply chain's sustainable value added (SVA). Why? Total supply chain emissions consist of the majority of a manufacturing firm's carbon footprint,[10] which has typically only been looked at as a cost of doing business. This is only one measure of supply chain performance. In the near future, performance will include

---

[9]Mathews et al. (2008).
[10]Huang et al. (2009).

multiple measures of financial, AND environmental, AND social performance taking firms beyond pollution prevention and into the realms of clean technology, product stewardship, and a sustainability vision.

Self-assessment at the Corporate Level

Assessment at a micro level enables understanding of business processes and elements of your business model (capabilities, key customer, and value proposition). We suggest internal assessment of your own function first. Start with a narrow scope or processes to assess. With an understanding of how you would approach this process from a single functional perspective, then move toward cross-functional involvement through the assembly of a team. This assessment process, when part of action learning, is best facilitated with the help of a cross-functional team. The audit and assessment process (for a single function or across functions) should have the goal of understanding:

- Performance metrics currently in use, assessment of pollution prevention.
- Best practices and integrated management systems.
- Interrelationships of processes and systems as a whole.
- GHG emission inventory and carbon footprint.
- Sustainable value added.
- Integration and design opportunities.
- New goals and metrics relative to sustainability opportunities and standards.
- Vision of the "To Be" state (carbon neutrality, zero emissions) and a sustainability vision.
- Integration into the day-to-day life of the firm.

Approach the self-assessment, opportunity identification, and change management through the use of Juran's Universal Breakthrough Sequence (UBS) reviewed in Chapter 4. As we know, Juran developed a systematic approach to TQM. The goal, in developing this approach, was to make quality into a habit. For quality to become a habit, it had to be the result of a repeatable process. This UBS process logic applies equally well to sustainability as a focal point as it applies to the proven benefits of TQM. The steps in this UBS process are within a context of self-assessment and proven practices including:

1. Proof of the need.
2. Project Identification.
3. Organization to guide each project.
4. Diagnosis—breakthrough in knowledge.
5. Remedial action on the findings.
6. Breakthrough in cultural resistance.
7. Control at the new level.

Outcomes of the self-assessment allow a team of internal managers to learn more about SSCM impacts across functions and its potential within the organization. Teams need to select and implement the most cost-effective technologies and practices. There is one caveat to the assessment. To help ensure a better outcome, assemble the team and perform the assessment without adding more responsibilities to team members' existing workloads. Thus, find a balance with the new initiative and lessening of prior responsibilities. We can all find some less valuable responsibilities we would like to get rid of, now is your chance.

Self-assessment at the Micro Level

Much of the traditional view of change management has focused on the prior two levels. That is, it is assumed that if the need for change is accepted at the macro and corporate levels, then the rest of the organization will go along with it. While this perspective is attractive (because it deals directly with the need for things such as top management support), it is also short-sighted. It assumes that the other organizational levels have little or no impact on the acceptance and diffusion of sustainability; it also implicitly assumes that there are no interactions between the levels. Both of these assumptions are wrong.

To be successful, sustainability and its need must be embraced by the people charged with deploying it. It must be accepted by the people who work on the shop floor. It must be embraced by the organizational buyers when contracts are awarded and when performance of the supply base is evaluated. It must be embraced by the packaging engineers when they design new packaging. It must become part of the organizational culture. It must become something that the people charged with deploying sustainability do naturally and consistently—even when the boss is not around. This is one reason that exemplar organizations such as Unilever are so successful when it comes to sustainability.

As pointed previously in this book on implementation, it is wrong to assume that users are additive thinkers. That is, when introducing sustainability, managements brings in new approaches and then proceeds to show that these approaches not only work but that they can work in their organizations. It is then assumed that the users will add these tools to the existing set and use them when necessary. The problem with this approach is that it is wrong. Users tend to be substitutive thinkers. That is, they will only drop existing tools and approaches when it is convincingly shown that the current ways of doing things is wrong and doomed. That is why crises are so effective—they show everyone in the organization that the current approaches are wrong and that they are no longer working. Unfortunately, the problem with crises is that there is a lack of time and a lack of resources needed to bring about change.

What this means is that when beginning the sustainability journey, management must spend time understanding the problems being addressed in the deployment areas and they must understand what tools are being used and why they are being used. Next, management must develop a strategy for convincingly discrediting the existing tools, if they are not in line with the goals of sustainability. Once the existing tools have been discredited, the new tools can be introduced. These will be more likely to be accepted because they are filling what has become an organizational vacuum.

Finally, it is important to recognize that since many of these tools and approaches are new, management must expect failure and it must be tolerant of failure. It must differentiate between *smart* failures and *dumb* failures. A dumb failure is when the employee does something that they have been told not to do—they essentially break the rules. Such failures should be punished if appropriate. Smart failures, in contrast, occur when the rules and procedures are implemented correctly and something unexpected occurs. Such failures should not be punished. If punished, the result is a clear message to the organization and its suppliers—DO NOT EXPERIMENT; DO NOT FAIL. When this message is sent out and accepted, there is no experimentation. Experimentation is critical if we are to be successful. Remember what turtles teach us—a turtle only advances when it sticks its neck out.

Action Items

One outcome for the assessment team should always be to educate others as to the meaning of, and opportunities for SSCM. One purposeful approach to educating yourself and others is found within the end of chapter Action Items (AIs). Each chapter in this book synthesizes information from the field and provides the reader with actionable insight for continuous improvement. AIs at the end of each chapter will help to identify and prioritize opportunities for action learning and organizational improvement.

Have the assessment team provide independent assessment from their own functional perspective as to what is important and why. Use our online assessment AIs to provide summary information of your assessment and within-industry comparisons as this is available to you at no cost. When the team has results, share the insight within the team and then widely within the organization. Create a sense of urgency and work toward quick wins where the results of the initiative(s) can be shared across functions.

Top Management Support

Support from the top is the key to any initiative. The need for SSCM project is recognized by everyone in the organization when it is evident that this initiative is being driven by top management's desire to improve the firm's competitive position or as a top management response to specific threats to the firm. In some cases, top management will initiate the program directly. In other cases, ad hoc groups already working on supplier issues initiate the need for a program. The recognition of the need for an initiative is then transformed into a set of organizational and sustainable objectives. These objectives can include the hiring of new talent from top MBA programs who are signatories to the United Nations Principles for Responsible Management Education (PRME), ranked by the Aspen Institute's Beyond Grey Pinstripes or the Corporate Knights Global Green MBA ranking of graduate business programs integrating sustainability within curriculum or highlighted in the Princeton Review's guide to green colleges. Objectives should be broad-based and flexible while balancing the ability of personnel to try new things and fail without retaliation. A culture of innovation cannot come about through a fear of failure. Finally, top management can make the UBS better established as the approach to SSCM opportunity identification and execution as part of internal reward and incentive systems.

Vision and Goals

A vision and goals should be the objective of the assessment team, including the steps and suppliers to include in this change process. A difficulty in doing this comes from how people in different parts of the organization talk about initiatives. Top management tends to focus on the bottom line while line workers talk about materials and resources. Thus, a vision helps to get people focused on the "To Be" state of the future. To this end, the opening chapter of the book Natural Capitalism[11] begins with:

> "Imagine for a moment a world where cities have become peaceful and serene because cars and buses are whisper quiet, vehicles exhaust only water vapor, and parks and greenways have replaced unneeded urban freeways. OPEC has ceased to function because the price of oil has fallen to five dollars a barrel, but there are few buyers for it because cheaper and better ways now exist to get the services people once turned to oil to provide."

The authors go on to talk about buildings that generate more electricity than they consume, atmospheric CO_2 levels decreasing for the first time in 200 years, water leaving facilities being cleaner than when it entered, and industrialized countries reducing resource consumption by

---

[11]Hawkins et al. (2008).

80 percent while improving the quality of life. This is only part of the first paragraph, yet it provides a vivid vision of the future and through back-casting (application of The Natural Step) from that vision to where we are today, it also provides an opportunity for decision makers to pause and think about how business processes and whole supply chains will have an impact on the Natural Capitalism vision.

With the help of top management, and the results of the assessment team's findings, the vision should be communicated widely, and aligned with training and resource allocation to make the initiative successful. The shared vision and performance metrics will bring the supply chain together as stakeholders will want to know how to create value while aligning processes and practices with the vision.

Sustainability is part of a mixed bag of outcomes . . . innovation, waste reduction, culture, visibility, value creation, and transparency across a supply chain. It is imperative to understand how it aligns with other systems and outcomes the organization is pursuing.

Three additional points must be reinforced before we leave this discussion of how to implement SSCM. First, involve your supply chain but do not expect the supply chain to believe that you are committed to sustainability until they see significant, verifiable evidence of progress within your organization.

Second, when undertaking change, first allow your people the opportunity to state their reservations and concerns. A great deal of organizational resistance to change is due to the fact that the people have valid concerns that they feel they are being ignored. Listen, understand, and work with the people to deal with these concerns.

Third, develop and maintain a sense of urgency. Often, these initiatives die because the people involved do not see them as being of high priority. Develop a timeline for change; identify and monitor milestones and progress; hold people accountable for results; report the good and the bad results; and be prepared to revise objectives and project timelines as events change. Develop and maintain an on-going pressure for change—a message that should be consistently delivered at all level of the organizations, beginning with the CEO. To this end, it is useful to look at what Unilever and Paul Polman has done—his timeline is a template that many firms should strive to emulate.

The future of SSCM, planning, and implementation all require management to take note of emerging trends and evidence of companies already engaged in these efforts. To this end, we have tried to revel how sustainability is becoming an order winner and competitive advantage for some.

Summary

The future of supply chain management will involve financial, AND environmental, AND social performance in addition to good governance practices throughout the life cycle of goods and services. As we have shown by the numerous examples in this chapter and previous chapters, innovative and early adopting companies are already driving sustainability internally and within their supply chains. With increased attention given to managing supply chain performance to an Integrated Bottom Line, there are frameworks such as the framework for strategic sustainable development (FSSD) (Chapter 2), and numerous practices and tools available to help you when planning and implementing SSCM.

Applied Learning: Action Items (AIs)—Steps you can take to apply the learning from this chapter

After reviewing this chapter, you should be ready to assess planning and implementation opportunities. To aid you in this assessment, please consider the following questions:

AI: Is the sustainability of our products limited by our own capabilities?

AI: Does our vision direct us toward solving social and environmental problems?

AI: Does our vision guide the development of new technologies, products, or processes for critical customers?

AI: What goals and metrics are already in use, and what new goals should be utilized relative to sustainability?

AI: What level of support can you garner for sustainability initiatives from top management?

Further Readings

Carbon Disclosure Project & Accenture (2012). Reducing Risk and Driving Business Value. *Supply Chain Report.*

Hart, S. L. (1997). Beyond Greening: Strategies for A Sustainable World. *Harvard Business Review.* 75(1)p. 66+

Laszlo, C. (2015). *Sustainability for Strategic Advantage: The Shift to Flourishing* Stanford University Press and Greenleaf Publishing.

Orts, E., & Spigonardo, J. (2012). *Greening the Supply Chain: Best Practices and Future Trends, Initiative for Global Environmental Leadership.*

Schein, E. H. (1999). The Corporate Culture Survival Guide: Sense and Nonsense about Culture Change. San Francisco, Calif: Jossey-Bass.

CHAPTER 6

Implementing Successful Sustainable Supply Chains to Drive Value

- On a quarterly basis, managers at DHL assess the impact of future scenarios and evaluate the opportunities and risks in their departments. The management process is used to assess environmental management risk. DHL services include reports on the carbon emissions arising from products and services used by their customers, and assessment of a customer's carbon footprint. Global Forwarding Freight also offers a "Carbon Dashboard." In addition to reports on carbon emissions, the dashboard simulates alternative supply chains combined with a carbon efficiency analysis.
- Based on information from 2,415 companies, including 2,363 suppliers and 52 major purchasing organizations who are Carbon Disclosure Project (CDP) Supply Chain program members, 70 percent of companies believe that climate change has the potential to affect their revenue significantly, a risk which is intensified by a chasm between the sustainable business practices of multinational corporations and their suppliers. These members include Dell, L'Oréal, and Walmart and represent a combined spending power of around US$1 trillion. The research marks CDP's most comprehensive annual update on the impact of climate change on corporate supply chains.[1]

---

[1]Carbon Disclosure Project and Accenture (2012).

The vignettes above provides a snapshot of the size and number of organizations already involved in implementing sustainability into supply chain management. Leading firms and NGOs are already measuring and integrating sustainability into performance measurement and strategic planning activities. The CDP recognizes greenhouse gas (GHG) emissions and carbon as a measure of this waste and an opportunity for improvement that will have many benefits outside of reducing emissions. If we sit back and think about what thousands of firms are already starting to do, then it becomes even more apparent that we need to understand the foundations of supply chain management, how business models are changing, performance metrics, design and measures of success in place to keep driving value.

Objectives

1. Review the foundations of sustainable supply chain management (SSCM, a synthesis of Volumes 1 and 2).
2. Enable action learning and applied approach to using the information in this book.

Foundations of Successful SSCM and Change Management

Supply chain strategies and practices have evolved from a typically noncompetitive, overlooked element of strategy before the 1980s, to a synergistic and integral part of corporate competitive advantage today. For firms who are considered to be Innovators and Early Adopters, there are many challenges and hidden opportunities to recognizing and integrating SSCM. We know that suppliers are critical to the competitive success of firms. The fact that future supplier performance is expected to continuously improve and involve new attributes of performance adds to the complexity of the function and the importance of the supply chain management professional. These decision makers will need to understand several foundational elements of SSCM to then be able to leverage these elements internally and externally, when working with their supply chain.

Sustainability as a system's approach is built on a number of premises (Table 6.1), as summarized in Volume 1, Chapter 1. Systems thinking is

Table 6.1 Foundations of Sustainable Supply Chain Management

- Focus on the 3Ps—product/process/packaging
- Prevention is preferred to correction
- Sustainability must be integrated into the day-to-day life of the firm
- Sustainability must be captured within strategic, tactical, and operational performance
- Sustainability is a system opportunity
- Sustainability must be linked to the strategy and the bottom line
- Waste is a symptom, not the root cause
- Waste is ultimately linked to processes
- Waste elimination and management is economically driven

an important part of this approach while understanding that each element contributes to the creation of value and success of larger systems such as a supply chain. These foundational elements include the following:

Recognition of these elements is an important first step in seeing your business system as a whole. To do this, attention should next turn to integrative models.

Understand Your Business Model

The business model is highly integrative bringing together the three elements of the key customer, the value proposition, and capabilities. As we know, capabilities, while important, are not enough by themselves. As capabilities change due to technological innovation, new tools, capital investments, and process improvements, these changes have to be evaluated in terms of how they affect the other two dimensions. If the firm targets sustainability initiatives as a way to attract a new key customer, it must reevaluate the appropriateness of the current value proposition and capabilities. The highest level of value is delivered when key customer expectations (recognized as order winners, and order losers, order qualifiers) are addressed by the value proposition and delivered by the capabilities of the firm.

Transparency

This is most notable through the broad expansion of corporate reporting. Sustainability reporting is the practice of measuring, disclosing, and being accountable to internal and external stakeholders for organizational performance toward the goal of sustainable development. Emerging companies like icix (www.icix.com) convene collaborative commerce networks allowing you to share information with your business partners and supply chain via the cloud.[2] They have 200 databases within their network and have plans to assess over 30,000 suppliers on sustainability and water use while also tracking dozens of interrelated performance indices.

Sustainability reporting describes the reporting of economic, environmental, and social impacts (e.g., an integrated bottom line, corporate responsibility reporting, and so on.).[3] A sustainability report should provide a balanced and reasonable representation of the sustainability performance of a reporting organization—including both positive and negative outcomes. To this end, we see the need for decision makers to view value creation in a new way. In Volume 1, chapter 2, we proposed building on the concepts of economic value added and total cost of ownership to now start assessment of sustainable value added (SVA). This will not be easy, but is a trend in the movement toward corporate reporting of an integrated bottom line.

SVA = Level of Financial, AND Environmental, AND Social Value
    Generated – Total Waste

Performance Metrics

Metrics are important to measure, monitor, and manage toward continuous improvement. Of the many types of metrics presented in Volume 1, Chapter 3, predictive metrics increase your chance of achieving a certain objective or goal in the future. Predictive metrics are associated with aspects of the process that are thought to affect the outcomes of interest. Predictive metrics are appropriate when the interest is in preventing the occurrence of problems, rather than correcting them.

---

[2]Touw (2012).
[3]Global Reporting Initiative (2013b).

Standards

Standards play an important role in a sustainable supply chain and can be used to achieve a number of important outcomes. These outcomes include financial, AND environmental, AND social performance. As such, standards should be leveraged for their alignment with a given business model and used carefully. There are a large (and ever growing) number of standards appropriate to sustainability along with a process for the appropriate usage and implementation of standards with over 30 of the most used standards outlined in Volume 1, Chapter 4.

A Management Toolkit

Tools enable decision makers to better assess processes and understand whole systems. The tools outlined in Chapter 4 focus on process flow analysis, major quality management tools, the plan-do-check-act (PDCA) cycle, and the opportunity to leverage multicriteria decision analysis to help assess new initiatives that do not have all the quantitative data you would like and can accommodate both qualitative and quantitative assessments of options involving more than one criterion of performance.

Designing Products and Processes

Design for Sustainability (DfS) and design thinking approach to any product or process refers to the methods and processes for investigating ill-defined problems, acquiring information, analyzing, and positing solutions early in the design and planning process. As described in Chapter 1, this design approach is a perfect fit for proactively minimizing waste and impacts of processes on larger systems. With this insight, managers can focus on the way that a system's parts interrelate and how systems work within the context of larger systems (also called systems thinking). If we design products, processes, packaging, or service with the objective of eliminating waste within systems, we will be well on our way to SSCM.

Life Cycle Assessment (LCA)

This technique is used to assess the environmental aspects and potential impacts associated with a product, process, packaging, or service. LCA is also a tool enabling DfS. There are numerous software packages and LCA tools available to help get started. The overall approach will involve first developing the goal, scope, and bounds of the assessment. The steps involved include (a) compiling an inventory of relevant energy and material inputs and environmental releases; (b) evaluating the potential environmental impacts associated with identified inputs and releases; and finally, (c) interpreting the results to help you make a more informed decision as to product, process, or packaging modifications. The interpretation of results should inform the decision-making process to lesson environmental impacts and associated costs. If you do not take this type of information into account, someone else may end up providing an LCA of your product on a website such as Sourcemap.com where transparency is taken to a new level.

Supply Chain Integration

Integration is critical to the success of any sustainability initiative. Recent findings from MIT Sloan and the Boston Consulting group find "Sustainability-driven Innovators do not treat sustainability as a standalone function detached from the business. They integrate their efforts into operations and planning.":[4] Integration occurs at various levels: legal, processes, data, systems, information flows, and the extent to which the participants invest in each other's systems. Integration ideally is found at the level of parties working closely together to ensure that their actions and flows are continuously synchronized. Integration is important because it influences visibility, the ease of information sharing, and the resulting supply chain relationship. This integration, visibility, and now its extension to traceability continue to grow in importance as organizations such as the United Nations Global Compact, with a task force of industry partners, are developing systems for tracing product and raw materials through complex global supply chains.

---

[4]MIT Sloan Management Review and Boston Consulting Group (2013).

One example of how transportation firms are coping with supplier integration and performance can be found within DHL, where subcontracted transportation accounts for most of the DHL Group's carbon emissions. Because of this, DHL has made managing subcontractors a key component of environmental protection programs. Determining the carbon performance of third-party transport providers is difficult and they have joined forces with Beiersdorf, Heineken, IKEA, La Poste, Procter & Gamble, TNT, UPS, as well as other international companies to found the Green Freight Europe initiative.[5] The goal is to increase transparency in the road freight segment by setting up a standardized system for collecting and reporting CO_2 emissions from road freight transport. The aim is to get all companies along the supply chain involved in the green procurement of transport services by offering improved transparency and comparability for carbon efficiency.

As we review the foundations of SSCM, they provide a road map for both short-term and long-term implementation opportunities for any organization. Next, we review how you will know when efforts can be deemed successful?

Measures of Success

Field research involving sustainability professionals within several large multinational corporations can be found within Chapters 2, as we revealed insight as to how they operationalized sustainability and work with supply chain managers. Their primary focus was on performance measurement, external rankings, and sustainability reporting.[6] When discussing the importance of measurement, participants highlighted setting goals and Key performance indicators (KPIs) as the most important enablers of understanding if operations and processes are progressing toward sustainability goals. As was mentioned by these professionals numerous times, sustainability should be everyone's responsibility and demonstration of this can be found in these organizations meeting and exceeding goals while tracking KPIs. What makes new initiatives successful is a combination of

---

[5]DHL (2011).
[6]Sroufe et al. (2012).

leadership, short-term and long-term projects, a road map, and compensation tied to performance of environmental and social initiatives. The most frequently noted metrics discussed by those interviewed include:

1. Energy efficiency.
2. GHG emissions.
3. Water consumption.
4. Solid waste.
5. Product attributes.
6. Environmental exposure.
7. Benchmarking external indices annually.
8. Carbon indexed to products and revenue.

Rankings are currently leveraged by sustainability professionals to validate practices and demonstrate programs going beyond compliance. The three primary rankings or indices highlighted in order of frequency are: Newsweek, the CDP, and the Dow Jones Sustainability Index. If your firm is included in these rankings, you are already considered to be among the Innovators and Early Adopters of sustainability practices and you are already producing a corporate sustainability report.

The global reporting initiative (GRI) is highlighted as the leading approach to measuring and disclosing information within corporate reports. Other important highlights include the use of integration of financial, environmental, and social reporting of performance, and the ISO certification also demonstrating assurance of performance within known standards.

If you think reporting is not yet a big deal consider the following. The GRI, Global Initiative for Sustainability Ratings (GISR), and the International Integrated Reporting Council (IIRC) have combined efforts to create a collaborative framework for integrated reporting and the convergence of financial and Environmental Social and Governance (ESG) information. These organizations are now supported by B Lab's, the Sustainability Accounting Standards Board (SASB) efforts, and Forum for the Futures Sustainable Business Model Group. Within the next few years, there will be a unified set of material criteria to rate and rank a firm's progress toward being a sustainable organization relative to its peers.

The trends of integration and transparency are supported by surveys and empirical evidence.[7] Consider what is already happening in other regions of the global marketplace: The Hong Kong stock exchange is now making ESG disclosure a best practice. Integrated reporting is now mandatory by the Johannesburg Stock Exchange and the King III Code of Corporate Governance in South Africa as they now have one of the highest reporting ratios of carbon accounting and integrated reporting.

Develop a Culture of Sustainability

Whether or not you are successful with developing and maintaining SSCM depends to large extent on whether the people in the organization accept and believe in sustainability initiatives. In many cases, this means making sustainability part of the corporate culture.

Organizations affect how their members see issues, deal with problems, and identify what is important. People are influenced by organizational goals, structure, training, coworker's attitudes, successes and failures, and a host of other aspects of organizational life. Operational programs such as those we have discussed in this book can have large impacts on organizational culture, and different cultures may be more or less appropriate for a given set of goals. For example, the organizational culture that evolves over time in a lean system emphasizes waste and variance reduction, along with process standardization and discipline. Such an approach may seem stifling to employees that are rewarded for radical innovations. In this way, operational initiatives can greatly affect the culture and work life of employees. Managers must often address conflicts between changing organizational goals and existing cultural norms. In fact, preexisting cultural norms often form serious impediments to organizational change. This is why in environments of rapid change, operations managers have to be so attuned to the strengths and weaknesses of their organization's culture. These strengths and weaknesses are often difficult to identify. As one manager put it, "organizational culture is what the employees do when the boss is not around."

---

[7]KPMG (2011).

While culture can be difficult to change, it can also be a key source of competitive advantage. For example, consider the success of Apple. Many people believe that the reason that Apple has been successful is because it has developed a culture of innovation.

Organizational culture is an increasingly important issue as operations managers seek to integrate partners in the supply chain. Culture affects supply-chain-related issues like trust and compliance. In general, the people in an organization work most comfortably with others who they perceive to be like them. They tend to be less trusting when dealing with people who are perceived to have different goals or motivations. For this reason, managers have to carefully consider differences in the organizational cultures of potential partners, and reassess current partners before they enter into long-term collaborative agreements.

Organizational culture plays a critical role in achieving sustainability goals. People within the organization must embrace and support the organization's view of sustainability in order for goals to be met. This is not always easy. There is disagreement and controversy surrounding some sustainability issues (global warming, for example). Leadership plays an important role in defining the culture and related sustainability goals. For example, Herman Miller of Zeeland, Michigan (a furniture company), has had extensive success with sustainability. One of the founders of Herman Miller believed strongly in corporate stewardship and responsibility. In large part, the company's commitment to sustainability stems from the values and corporate culture created by this founding leader.

Consequently, to succeed with sustainability in the long term, sustainability must not be something that is discussed in annual reports or something that is pointed out to visiting governmental official. Rather, sustainability must become part of the organizational culture. It must become something that the employees do when the boss is not around.

Benefits of SSCM Practices

The benefits of sustainable supply management form the fundamental reason for undertaking the sustainability challenge and the next industrial revolution. It is not surprising that benefits include both direct and indirect financial benefits. The most commonly found benefits include: (a) a reduction of costs, including a product's whole life costs and the organization's overall operating costs; (b) increased competitive advantage; (c) increased profits; (d) decreased damage to the environment and human health, (e) increased levels of innovation, (f) the potential to gain new customer market segments, and (g) risk mitigation.

Understand that sustainability is an issue of managing perceptions of trade-offs. We know from Volume 1, Chapter 1, and Accenture that firms can simultaneously improve sustainability, AND cost effectiveness, AND service quality. [8] Once we leave the low-hanging fruit, we have to identify and deal with progressively more difficult decisions. The nice thing about low-hanging fruit is that due to changes in technology and innovation, it keeps growing back.[9]

Transforming the supply chain business model is the corporate strategy of the future. Because much of your firm's impacts are likely to be in your supply chain, it makes sense to integrate the supply chain as early as possible. Today, large companies, including more than 85 percent of the global 250, have or are developing sustainability reports with specific goals and targets. Many even have holistic "plans" with ambitious 2020 and 2050 targets across their business. Some are even combining annual financial and sustainability reporting. Making these plans happen, and capturing their impact internationally, is going to be about sustainable change in how supply chains operate. To make sustainability a reality, "technology providers, businesses, citizens and government will need to collaborate to develop the right policies and infrastructure that drive economic growth, and motivates sound behavior change and ensures the sustainability of our communities.[10]

If you need further evidence of what is happening, consider the efforts of one large multinational, MillerCoors.

---

[8]Accenture (2009).

[9]Lovins and Cohen (2011).

[10]Henretig (2012). Also see Reinventig Fire by Lovins A. and the Rocky Mountain Institute for examples of how this is already being done.

Sustainability in Action: MillerCoors Makes Making Brew Sustainable

To understand how all of these elements fit together, consider the experiences of MillerCoors. MillerCoors is a major American-based alcoholic beverage brewing and marketing company. It is a company with a long history in the making and marketing of beer. Its products are known and respected within the market. Yet, for MillerCoors, the last 15 years have been a period of extreme turbulence and change. These changes fall into one of three categories:

- Ownership: It has moved from being an independent company to being part of the Molson family and now it is part of SAB Miller.;
- Marketing: MillerCoors has traditionally seen itself as a company selling a "blue collar" beer—that is, a beer that is drunk primarily by working people. However, these are being increasingly replaced by millennials. The common definition of a millennial is any person born between 1982 and 2002. These consumers began arriving into the marketplace in 2003. What MillerCoors quickly found was that these consumers saw things differently as compared to its traditional consumer base. Specifically, these consumers brought with them a new set of attitudes. It was not enough to offer these buyers a good product. What these consumers wanted were products to be responsibly produced. In the case of beer, this meant that they were concerned about the sustainability of the process used in making the product. They were concerned about the amount of water used in making the beer; they were concerned about the impact of the company of the communities, either directly (through the disposal of waste water) or indirectly (through drunkenness). They were also concerned about whether the company offered real opportunities for advancement and promotion in the management for women and minorities.
- Competition: MillerCoors found itself faced by flat sales in its mainline beer products. There were main reasons. First, there was the advent of micro and craft brewers that were able to offer new and different drinking experiences. Second, competition with its

traditional competitors had increased due in part to consolidation within the traditional brewing industry. Third, MillerCoors was seeing competition from new forms of alcoholic beverages. In addition to hard liquors and malt beverages, MillerCoors was experiencing competition from new forms such as flavored ciders and meads (honey-based wines).

These forces were sufficient to get the management at MillerCoors to reconsider their current strategies and reporting. Initially, they focused on a strategy of sustainability as waste management. This made a great deal of sense. After all, making beer was a very water-intensive process. Craft brewers found that for every gallon of beer that they produced, they used between 6 and 10 gallons of water. In addition, some of MillerCoors' breweries were located in the arid Southwest of the United States—areas where water was scarce.

Consequently, MillerCoors focused on reducing waste. It would use less water per gallon of beer; the water that it returned to the local watersheds would be of better quality than the water that it had used. It would reduce packaging. Audits were carried out, measures developed and posted, extensive efforts were made to recruit and maintain top management support.

Yet, it quickly became evident that there was more to sustainability. It was quickly evolving into a broad-based strategic initiative that involved more than the making of beer; it involved the communities in which Miller-Coors products were being consumed; it also involved the supply chain.

Community Outreach: MillerCoors recognized the irresponsible usage of its products could hurt people, families, and communities. This usage took two forms: underage drinking and excessive drinking. Regarding the first form, MillerCoors has worked with local communities to stamp out underage drinking through numerous campaigns. On the second form, MillerCoors has encouraged responsible drinking through its Drink Responsibly program. It also introduced a program for the destined drivers—one that rewards them with free beverages and in some communities a chance to enter a drawing where they can win a new truck.

The Supply Chain: The supplier base presented MillerCoors with some of its most interesting challenges. Here, the focus was on the suppliers of the grains and various ingredients used in making beer. When MillerCoors explored its supply chain, it found that many of its suppliers were small, family-owned operations. As MillerCoors began to work with these farmers, certain lessons emerged.

First, since these suppliers were small, they often lacked the resources needed to achieve the objectives of reducing waste. This forced MillerCoors to recognize that it had to change its role and responsibility. It could not simply mandate the outcomes and have the suppliers be held responsible for achieving them. Rather, it had to act as an advisor, coach, and as a source of information. It had to work with its suppliers, educating them on what was and was not possible. It had to do a great deal of research and then be willing to share its findings and insights with its suppliers. It had to be patient and wait until its suppliers began to understand what is sustainability, how to achieve and then began to see the results.

In the process of working with its suppliers, MillerCoors began to realize the importance of organizational culture. It found that its efforts with sustainability were most successful when the suppliers that they were working with also valued and embraced sustainability as part of the organization's core values. This awareness also helped to make MillerCoors sensitive to the need to embed sustainability within the organization culture at MillerCoors. That is, it would be wrong to establish a sustainability department and then have that department manage all of the sustainability activities. That approach would effectively isolate sustainability and create a "that's not my job mentality." Rather, sustainability had to become part of the day-to-day life of everyone at MillerCoors; it had to become integral to the core values of MillerCoors. If successful, culture would act as a multiplier for sustainability efforts. As a result, the team responsible for implementing sustainability began the long process of starting to embed sustainability within the core value of MillerCoors. This process was greatly simplified by top management's decision to embrace sustainability and to transform it from a waste reduction program to a strategic business model initiative.

MillerCoors is expanding its work on sustainability to include its management ranks. One of its goals is to ensure that by 2020, at least 43 percent of its management workforce consists of minorities and women.

What is interesting about this story is that it really embodies many of the lessons and guidelines presented in this chapter. In a move to better inform stakeholders, MillerCoors also produces a GRI sustainability report using G4 guidelines. It shows how a company can quickly turn itself around and become more sustainable not only within the organization but also within the supply chain.

Summary

Understanding sustainability is only the first step in integrating this paradigm into your own organization. We have tried to concisely provide guidelines, tools, examples, and frameworks for integration and implementation. The experiences of MillerCoors as they progressed with its sustainability journey highlight what only a few years ago some have said could not be done, making operations and supply chains more sustainable. This book can be considered a synthesis of information providing a go-to resource for managers struggling with the overwhelming amount of information about sustainable business practices. It can also be used as evidence of change, proof to counter those who say it cannot be done, and examples showing the ability of some to cross the sustainability chasm into the development of more sustainable supply chains.

Our approach in developing this book has been to help decision makers in their search for answers to questions concerning sustainability, business models, drivers of value creation, and implementation of sustainable business practices within operations and supply chain management. We hope you find our approach useful and engaging as in the next chapter we conclude Volume 2 by looking at the future of SSCM and important trends.

Further Readings

Lovins, A., & The Rocky Mountain Institute (2011). *Reinventing Fire-Bold Business Solutions for The New Energy Era*. Chelsea Green Publishing, White River Junction Vermont.

United Nations Global Compact and Business for Social Responsibility (2015). *Supply Chain Sustainability: A Practical Guide for Continuous Improvement.*(2nd edition): https://www.unglobalcompact.org/docs/issues_doc/supply_chain/SupplyChainRep_spread.pdf - accessed February 23, 2017.

Schein, E. H. (2010). Organizational Culture and Leadership. San Francisco: Jossey-Bass

Hahn, T., Preuss, L., Pinkse, J., & Figge, F. (2014). Cognitive Frames in Corporate Sustainability: Managerial Sensemaking With Paradoxical and Business Case Frames. Academy of Management Review, *39*(4), 463–487.

CHAPTER 7

Sustainable Supply Chain Management—The End of the Beginning

Run your business as if it's in trouble. Because if you don't, it will be some day.

—Jack Miles

The evolving sustainable supply chain management paradigm.

Sustainability—Broadened, Integrated, Elevated

The *Guardian* (UK) noted that many of the world's biggest car makers—companies such as Vauxhall (UK), BMW, Volkswagen, and Audi—had launched investigations into their paint supply chains.[1] The reason—an article published by the *Guardian* that linked many of their paint supply chains (and their demand for mica) to illegal mines in India where child labor and debt bondage was widespread. In fact, according to this article, children as young as 10 years old were being used to extract mica—the mineral that made car paint shimmer—from the ground and to sort it. This was dangerous, hard labor. In many cases, the children were working at the mines rather than going to school because their families needed the money.

Three Indian exporters—Mohan Mica, Pravin, and Mount Hill—seemed to be the major transgressor. These companies, in turn, sold their raw materials to customers such as Fujian Kancai, a company whose customers included cosmetics giant L'Oreal, P&G, PPG, and Axalta (the last two customers are leading car paint suppliers in a 19 billion USD world car paint maker). As a result of this report, Vauxhall (part of the GM group), BMW, and Volkswagen have launched investigations into their paint supply chains in response to the *Guardian* article, since this finding, if supported, is against company policies that explicitly prohibits such practices.

This article is important for several reasons. First, it shows that the power of the media can identify problems involving sustainability and make these immediately apparent to a wide audience. Second, companies are now recognizing the linkages between sustainability and risk. Failure to be sustainable can be the source of supply chain risk; it can affect the ability of the firm to serve its key customers; it can adversely affect the firm from an operational, strategic, and reputation perspectives. Third, because of this linkage, firms are now increasingly integrating sustainability into their enterprise risk management systems (ERMS). As will be shown later on in this chapter, this integration is important as it sends a clear message to the rest of the organization and to its supply chain, namely:

---

[1] P. Bengtsen & A. Kelly, (2016). Vauxhall and BMW among car firms linked to child labor over glittery mica paint. *The Guardian.* (July 28, 2016). file:///E:/SMR%20-%20Risk /Vauxhall%20and%20BMW%20among%20car%20firms%20linked%20to %20child%20labour%20over%20glittery%20mica%20paint%20_%20Global %20development%20_%20The%20Guardian.pdf. Last viewed August 1, 2016.

- Sustainability is important!
- Problems in sustainability are a major form of supply chain risk since they can adversely affect the firm's ability to serve the needs of its customer base.
- Sustainability can no longer be managed as a stand-alone activity; it must be integrated into the formal corporate management system.
- Given the importance of supply chain risk, issues involving supply chain risk are now being addressed at the top management level. By integrating sustainability into the ERMS, issues involving sustainability are becoming highly visible and conversely important to top management.
- This trend is not going away; if anything, it will increase in importance into the future.

This development was first observed by a research project entitled *Strategic Supply Chain Management—Beyond the Horizon* (BTH). This long-term project was aimed at identifying and exploring emerging issues in supply chain management both domestically and internationally. This project, jointly sponsored by Department of Supply Chain Management, the Eli Broad School of Business and APICs, has over a three-year span studied over 60 leading supply chain management organizations. The results and insights obtained from this project have been fine-tuned and tested in a series of focused workshops. One of the critical findings from this project was that (1) sustainability was identified as a major issue facing nearly every firm; and, (2) it was being integrated into the firm's risk management strategy.

Consequently, to understand these developments, it is first important to understand the concepts of supply chain risk and resilience. These two issues have been major issues since firms became aware of joint importance and their linkages. To a large extent, they were the same reasons why top management first became aware of the strategic importance of the supply chain.

Risk and Resilience—the Current State

Since the lightning strike and the subsequent fire at the Philips plant in March 2000 in Albuquerque, New Mexico, managers and researchers have come to realize the hidden cost and danger of supply chain management—that of interdependency and supply chain risk. Thanks to academic researchers, it is now known that a supply chain disruption, irrespective of its source, can reduce the stock price of the firm experiencing the disruption by up to 40 percent and that it can take up to two years to recover. Such findings have caused upper management to take the notion of supply chain risk very seriously and to develop systems for managing such risks. Managers have also come to recognize the need to develop the capacity to deal with such issues—a capacity that we now recognize as *resilience*.

Supply chain resilience is "the ability of a supply chain to both resist disruptions and recover operational capability after disruptions occur." When viewed from this perspective, resilience consists of two critical but complementary system components: the capacity for resistance and the capacity for recovery.

- Resistance capacity is the ability of a system to minimize the impact of a disruption by evading it entirely (*avoidance*) or by minimizing the time between disruption onset and the start of recovery from that disruption (*containment*).
- Recovery capacity is the ability of a system to return to functionality once a disruption has occurred. The process of system recovery is characterized by a (hopefully brief) *stabilization* phase after which a *return* to a steady state of performance can be pursued. The final achieved steady-state performance may or may not reacquire original performance levels, and is dependent on many disruption and competitor factors.

As we continue to draw on supply chain management and its various capabilities to reduce costs, reduce lead time, facilitate innovation, and enhance quality, we must improve our understanding of the complexity of supply chain risk. We are starting to recognize that it is a broader concept that encompasses more dimensions than bankruptcy, earthquakes, strikes, and fires.

More specifically, this broadening includes the consideration of sustainability as a risk and strategic opportunity. Firms are now recognizing that failure to ensure a sustainable supply chain can create risks for the supply chain and for the firm. That was the point of the *Guardian* story. As can be seen, sustainability is becoming integrated into the firm and its activities. It is no longer something that we should consider after everything else has been done.

Trends to Watch

Evidence of changing customer expectations and sustainability moving up the corporate agenda confirmed by a KPMG global survey of 378 senior executives[2] which found:

- 62 percent of firms surveyed have a strategy for corporate sustainability with 23 percent of firms in the process of developing a plan.
- Primary drivers for sustainability are resource and energy efficiency, with brand enhancement, regulatory policy, and risk management still remaining key drivers.
- 44 percent of executives in the study see sustainability as a source of innovation, whereas 39 percent see sustainability as a source of new business opportunity.
- Firms are increasingly measuring and reporting their sustainability performance and businesses want a successor to the Kyoto Protocol.
- 67 percent of executives believe a new set of rules is "very important" or "critical" to having a clear road map for sustainability with corporate-lobbying efforts pushing for tighter rules.

With increasing scrutiny of corporate carbon emissions, freight and transportation providers now have every opportunity to strategically impact and realize sustainable value from their operations. Emissions from freight in the United States are projected to increase by 74 percent from 2005 to 2035 and China is expected to increase its use of freight transportation fuels by 4.5 percent a year from 2008 to 2035 with predictions

---

[2]KPMG (2011).

of freight emissions increasing 40 percent globally.[3] Given this growth, we paradoxically have significant control over the carbon footprint of supply chain operations. Decisions on how products are designed and packaged, along with where products are made, store locations, offsetting, and how much time is allotted for transit all have an impact on greenhouse gas (GHG) emissions and waste within business systems. We should all have a strategy for corporate sustainability, its measurement, and how we will report our progress. Shippers will find that there are cleaner and more cost-efficient freight practices and integrated systems with good returns on investment. Sustainability is a way to differentiate operations, improve brand loyalty, provide new services, and, a road map for long-term goals.

With sights set on achieving more sustainable supply chains by 2020, objectives for some companies (i.e., the Consumer Goods Forum, HP, Microsoft, and others) include optimizing shared supply chains, engaging technologically savvy consumers, while also improving consumer health and well-being. The ability to achieve these objectives is essential to the consumer goods industry. It was noted that the difference between success and failure in this industry will be the ability to adapt to rapid and significant change. The trends with the biggest impact on driving industry objectives for the next 10 years include the following:

1. Increased urbanization.
2. Aging population.
3. Increasing spread of wealth.
4. Increased impact of consumer technology adoption.
5. Increase in consumer service demands.
6. Increased importance of health and well-being.
7. Growing consumer concern about sustainability.
8. Shifting of economic power.
9. Scarcity of natural resources.
10. Increase in regulatory pressure.
11. Rapid adoption of supply chain technology capabilities.
12. Impact of next-generation information technologies.

---

[3]KPMG (2011).

Within the context of these trends, industry needs a fundamental change in the way consumer products companies and retailers business models integrate issues such as sustainability for better serving consumers. This means working collaboratively with industry, governments, NGOs (non-governmental organizations), and consumers. The four primary objectives coming out of the study are (1) making business more sustainable, (2) optimizing a shared supply chain, (3) engaging with technology-enabled consumers, and (4) serving the health and well-being of consumers. Like the information technology and quality megatrends of the past, sustainability will touch every function, every business line, and every employee. Companies that excel in sustainability make corresponding shifts in leadership, the systematized use of tools, strategic alignment, integration, reporting, and communication. These firms move from tactical, ad hoc, and siloed approaches to strategic, systematic, and integrated practices.

Add to these trends the following recent events: the signing of the Climate Accord in Paris, release of the UN's 17 Sustainability Development Goals, toxic air in parts of China causing manufacturing to shut down or slow down, and the Pope's Laudato Si, and we need to ask ourselves a few questions. One, what new business leaders will emerge in this changing environment? Two, how will these leaders reorganize business as a vehicle for system change?

The Emerging Supply Chain Leader—Strategic in Focus

The emerging supply chain leader—such as those we encountered in the Beyond the Horizon Project and the one hinted at in the Deloitte supply chain survey—has a very different set of skills and orientations, namely:

Excels at managing at the interfaces. The new supply chain leader recognizes that they must work with other functions within the firm. Specifically, they must be prepared to engage with groups such as engineering, marketing, finance, accounting, and top management. This engagement is bidirectional. On one hand, they need to understand the requirements of these other groups since their needs have to be translated into capabilities that the supply chain must provide. On the other hand, the new supply chain leader must be prepared to educate these other groups on the capabilities of the supply chain—what the supply chain can and cannot do. They must also be able to communicate how actions taken by these other groups affect the performance of the supply chain. This capability is critical to sustainability since decisions made by people working in marketing or engineering can significantly affect the ability of the supply chain to achieve its sustainability objectives. A promotion may look like a great idea. However, we have to consider what to do with the products that we pull off the shelves and whether the demands of the promotion cause inefficient transportation moves. In other words, the new supply chain leader must excel at educating, integrating, and coordinating.

Focus on asking the "right" question, rather than on the "right" solution. This is where critical thinking shines. As Charles F. Kettering, the brilliant designer and engineer at General Motors, once said, "a problem well stated is a problem half solved." Here, the supply chain leader is more interested in ensuring that there is a clear and concise understanding of the desired outcome, rather than focusing on a specific solution. This means ensuring that everyone understands what the goal is, and then soliciting the input of the various members of the supply chain to identify how best to achieve this goal. The solution becomes secondary to the desired outcome because it is driven by this outcome. It is at this "right" question level that the new supply chain manager is able to ensure that everyone understands what is really critical. It is that this level that the discussions of sustainability must take place.

Strives for business excellence, rather than supply chain excellence. Here, the goal is to help the firm better compete at the business model rather than the supply chain level. This is important since our position in this book is that sustainability is a business issue rather than a supply chain issue.

Outside/In as compared to Inside/Out. A strategic supply chain manager views the capabilities of the supply chain through a different lens. The traditional lens is from the Inside/Out, where the leader understands what the supply chain can and cannot do and tries to convince key customers that this is what they really want. The new, strategic lens is from the Outside/In: It looks at what the key customers want and what type of outcomes they wish to achieve. These new leaders understand that it is these key customers who drive the firm, its strategy and ultimately the supply chain. This is critical since the new critical customer, in many cases, come from millennial. For this group, sustainability in its broadest form is critical. They are not interested in simply reducing pollution also in issues such as whether the workers operating in the supply chain were able to work in safe environments and whether or not they were paid a fair wage. It is this emphasis on the key customer, part of the outside/in approach, that explains the responses taken by car companies such as BMW, Volkswagen, and Vauxhall, to the presence of mica that was produced using child labor and debt bondage workers. This identification with key customers takes its most immediate form in terms of how communication is implemented—through measures and metrics.

Effective at communicating with others in terms of performance measurement. To effectively communicate within the firm, the new supply chain leader must recognize the importance of measures and metrics as communication. Measures and metrics, as noted by management experts Joan Magretta and Nan Stone, restate the business strategy and the business model into what each group or person must do to achieve this strategy. Increasingly, we are recognizing that effective communication within the firm occurs at this level, not in terms of measures such as capacity, throughput, utilization, and ppm. The new supply chain leader uses these measures to show how the actions of the supply chain can affect how others perform. Furthermore, in many cases, the new supply chain leader takes this emphasis on performance to a new level by adopting the customers' own measures as their own. When this occurs, communication is immediately enhanced between the supply chain and the customer since both are using the same set of measures. More importantly, supply chain impact can be seen immediately since these actions can be translated into how they affect the performance of the customer. Since both parties are using the same numbers (so to speak), the opportunity for conflict is minimized. We communicate through metrics and measure the totality of dimensions that we see as being part of sustainability—that sustainability is more than pollution reduction; it also embraces social sustainability.

Finally, it is good to remember a point that was raised in Volume 1 regarding metrics and measures—if you measure something such as sustainability, you are telling everyone that it is important; if you do not measure it, then it is unimportant and it can be ignored.

Recognizes the need for complexity but still strives to identify and eliminate complication. Since the new supply chain leader closely knows and identifies with the key customer, there is an acceptance of the need for complexity. Complexity is a trait that comes from the key customer and is something that the supply chain must be able to accommodate. Sustainability is inherently embedded in this complexity. The leader does try to communicate the downside risks of complexity through a cost of complexity approach (see Figure 7.1). However, the leader is able to differentiate between complexity, which comes from the customer, and a complication, which occurs because of the actions of people within the supply chain.

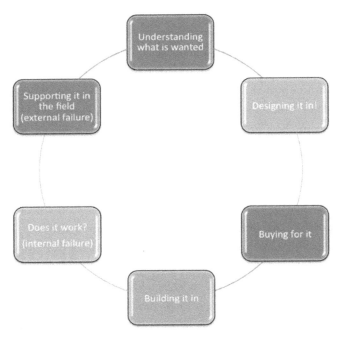

Figure 7.1 Cost of complexity—A total cost approach

As an example of a complication, consider the following situation. A firm has a short-term quality problem with a component supplier. To address the immediate issue, it modifies its manufacturing process to include an inspection activity. The problem is eventually addressed but the inspection is not removed. This inspection is an example of a complication—something that plagues most supply chain systems. The new supply chain leader may have a purpose to add complications, such as increasing the number of backup suppliers, but these actions are often driven by the need to protect the system from disruptions and to improve resilience.

Recognizes and accepts the presence of uncertainty and change. Uncertainty is viewed as the natural state of things when it comes to making a decision. After all, you never have enough time; the information is never complete or sufficiently accurate; and something is always changing before you make your decision.

Strives for robust rather than optimal systems. Optimality is nice. However, in many cases, optimality results in fragile systems. That is, as long as things have not changed from the conditions that were used to derive the optimal solution, all is well. However, as soon as something changes in the environment, the optimal system sputters. Instead, the goal should be a robust system, one that may not generate optimal performance but is able to respond to changes without extracting a severe penalty in performance. Robust systems are the natural complement to the preceding trait.

The focus is on the future. In this new environment of change and uncertainty, the past is viewed as a lesson to be learned, and not as the basis for punishment. As one manager in the Beyond the Horizon project put it, "The past is something you cannot do anything about. Learn from it; get over it; focus rather on the future." That is the attitude assumed by the new supply chain leader. This focus and concern about the past is also reflected in planning. The new supply chain leader recognizes the importance of that basic supply chain dictum—today's supply chain is the result of investments made in the past; tomorrow's supply chain will be the result of investments made today!

Fast decision making is the key. In this environment, you do not have the time to wait until changes shake out. Rather, you have to make decisions quickly and be willing to live with the fact that you will be wrong on occasion. This is becoming the natural state of affairs. As one manager put it, "you make decisions quickly, you fail fast, you learn quickly, you move on." This was best illustrated by one interview that took place at a fast fashion goods operation located in the Midwest during the Beyond the Horizon project. The manager who was leading research team members on a plant tour stopped to point out a new $1.7 million line. He asked the research team to guess how long it took to go from problem awareness to the time that this line was up and running. The team members answered with numbers ranging from two to three years. The response—7 months. When questioned, he brought out the key lesson—if the company had waited to make sure that the issue driving the need for the investment was real, it would have been too late. A new, faster method of decision making is demanded. In today's environment, fast decision making also means considering multiple factors such as sustainability as part of the decision-making process.

Sustainability is now an integral element of the decision-making process. Finally, sustainability in its broadest sense is no longer a separate issue—an issue that can be addressed after everything else has been looked at. It is no longer a constraint—something that must be satisfied as another objective. It is now a business requirement and part of the strategy by which the firm competes in the marketplace. It is a factor influencing how the supply chain is structured and determining who is qualified to be a supply chain supplier and who is not (as shown by the decision of Disney not to source products supplied from countries such as Pakistan and Bangladesh). It is also an opportunity for the firm to re-examine its processes and its supply chain for ways of doing things differently (think back to experiences of McCormick's and how it was able to develop suppliers in Uganda who could supply vanilla beans with the exact qualities needed by McCormick's).

The Challenge

The evidence, as summarized in Table 7.1 is clear. While there will always be a demand for tacticians and fire fighters, the new strategic supply chain

Table 7.1 Comparing Traditional Supply Chain Managers to the Leaders of the Future

Traits	Traditional Supply Chain Manager	Strategic Supply Chain Leader
Orientation	Functional; Strongly internal	Cross-boundary; Coordination
Performance stance	Cost/cost minimization; Environmental	Outcome-driven/revenue maximization; Integrate environmental AND social
Definition of excellence	Supply chain excellence	Business excellence
Stance	Focus on execution	Asking the right question Making sure the desired outcome is understood and made inevitable
Dealing with the customer	Inside/Out	Outside/In
Communication	Very functionally oriented Capacity, throughput, bottlenecks, inventory, ppm	Performance measures and metrics Use the customer's metrics as ours
Complexity	Strives to eliminate or simplify complexity	Accepts complexity as a fact of life that must be master Strives to elimination unnecessary complications
Uncertainty	Desires stability; manage change	Accepts uncertainty and change
Decision-making style	Deliberate	Fast decision making
Role of sustainability	A secondary issue Something that is considered after the other issues have been addressed A constraint	A business requirement—one of the desired outcomes that the supply chain can deliver An opportunity for improvement and for developing competitive advantage in the marketplace
Desired types of solutions	Optimal	Robust
Overall stance	Toolsmiths—masters of tools	Problem masters—define the problem that the rest of the supply chain will focus on

needs a different type of leader, perhaps a Chief Supply Chain Office (CSCO), who is well prepared by skills, temperament, and preparation to sit at the same table as the CEO, CIO, the CFO and the other similar leaders. What we are seeing from Table 7.1 is the emergence not of a supply chain manager but rather of the supply chain leader—someone who can think broadly and who can think critically.

The new supply chain leader must be one who is not simply willing to tolerate sustainability but who embraces it—recognizing it for what it truly is—part of the new skill set and requirements that the new supply chain leader is able to manager.

As can be seen from this chapter, sustainability is changing. It is now part of the present and the future for the supply chain manager. It is now helping to redefine the supply chain manager from being simply a manager to being a strategic leader. It is part of the changing landscape that is affecting not only the supply chain but also the firm and competition. As it changes, the result is that we are faced with three unresolved question—"Are you ready? Is your firm ready? Is your supply chain ready?" That is the challenge that this chapter will end with. It is also the challenge that authors wish to give you, the reader—ARE YOU READY?

In Conclusion, sustainable supply chain management is changing rapidly, faster than the rate at which global freight is moving, and every day, new developments shape our future in exciting ways. One of the objectives of this two book volume is to create a community of informed business professionals engaged in action learning, performance measurement, and the continuous improvement of sustainable business systems. We want to help you stay current with new developments. To this end, we hope you and your colleagues will discuss and revisit this book on a regular basis to engage and learn while working through chapter Action Items (AIs). Stay in touch with us to share your success stories' regarding what is, and is not working; to review benchmarking and audit information; and get access to current research. Together, we can shape the future of business, take action, and improve supply chain performance.

This book is just the first step toward action. To get the benefit of SSCM, join professional associations that engage in the development of sustainability in your profession. Talk to and work with sustainability professionals within and outside your organization. SSCM will be in continuous development, yet we need to break down the walls between functions and between practitioners and scholars. This is the beginning of the journey for all of us with the goal of sustainable business systems enabled by supply chain management that drives value. The journey is all part of a paradigm shift toward Integrated Bottom Line measurement and reporting with a better understanding of the value sustainability brings to any organization.

This is not the end of the beginning, but the beginning of the end of our time with you in the context of this book. We invite you to stay connected to this evolving paradigm and to participate in the journey that comes next.

> *Now this is not the end. It is not even the beginning of the end. But it is, perhaps, the end of the beginning.*
>
> —Winston Churchill

References

This list includes both references that were directly cited in this Volume and useful references. Any reference denoted by a *, if not directly cited in this text, is useful and it should be read because it contributes to a better understanding of the issues raised in this two Volume set regarding SSCM.

* 2020 Future Value Chain Project (2011). Retrieved March 22, 2013, from http:// www.futurevaluechain.com/

Accenture (2008). *The high performance supply chain study*. Published at www .accenture.com

Accenture (2009). *The sustainable supply chain*. Retrieved March 22, 2013, from http://www.accenture.com

Allenby, B. (1993). *Industrial Ecology*. New York, NY: Prentice Hall.

* Annie, L. (2007). *The story of stuff*. Retrieved March 22, 2013, from http://www .storyofstuff.org/

* Berthelot, S., Cormier, D., & Magnan, M. (2003). Environmental disclosure research: Review and synthesis. *Journal of Accounting Literature, 22*, 1–44.

Bhat, V. (1993). Green marketing begins with green design. *Journal of Business and Industrial Marketing, 8*(3), 26–31.

* Blackburn, W. (2007). Determining scope: An operational definition of sustainability, Chapter 2, *The Sustainability Handbook* (pp. 17–33). Environmental Law Institute.

Branchfeld, D., Dritz, T., Kodaman, S., Phipps, A., Steiner, E., & Keoleian, G. (2001). *Life Cycle Assessment of the Stonyfield Product Delivery System*. Ann Arbor: University of Michigan. Master's Thesis, CSS01-03.

* Bratt, C. (2014). Integrating a strategic sustainability perspective into eco-labeling, procurement, and supply chain management. Doctoral dissertation series No. 2014:06, Blekinge Institute of Technology, Department of Strategic Sustainable Development, Karlskrona, Sweden.

Braumguart, M., & McDonough, M. (2007). Cradle to cradle design: Creating healthy emissions—a strategy for eco-effective product and system design. *Journal of Cleaner Production, 15*, 1337–1348.

* Broman, G. I., & Robért, K.-H. (2017). A framework for strategic sustainable development. *Journal of Cleaner Production, 140*, 17–31.

* Brown, H. S., Martin D. J., & Teodorina L. (2007). *The rise of the Global Reporting Initiative (GRI) as a Case of Institutional Entrepreneurship*

(pp. 1–48). Harvard University. www.hks.harvard.edu. September 22, 2011. Retrieved March 22, 2013, from http://www.hks.harvard.edu/mrcbg/CSRI /publications/workingpaper_36_brown.pdf

* Craft, E. (2012). *Envisioning a smarter, healthier supply chain for shippers.* Published on GreenBiz.com. Retrieved October 19, 2012, from http://www .greenbiz.com/print/49054

* Carbon Disclosure Project (2011). Retrieved September 27, 2011, from https:// www.cdproject.net/en-US//Pages/overview.aspx

Carbon Disclosure Project & Accenture (2012). *Reducing risk and driving business value—DCP supply chain report.* Retrieved March 22, 2013, from https:// www.cdproject.net/CDPResults/CDP-Supply-Chain-Report-2013.pdf

Charan, P., Shankar, R., & Baisya, R. K. (2008). Analysis of interactions among the variables of supply chain performance measurement system implementation. *Business Process Manage Journal, 14*(4), 512–529.

* Chesbrough, H., & Rosenbloom, R. S. (2002). The role of the business model in capturing value from innovation: Evidence from Xerox Corporation's technology spin-off companies. *Industrial and Corporate Change, 11*(3), 529–555.

* Cone Communications, (2010). *Cause evolution study.* Retrieved March 22, 2013, from http://www.conecomm.com/2010-cone-cause-evolution-study

Cooper, R. (1993). *Winning at New Products: Accelerating the Process from Idea to Launch* (2nd ed). Boston: Addison-Wesley.

Curkovic, S., & Sroufe, R. P. (2011). Using ISO 14001 to promote a sustainable supply chain strategy. *Business Strategy and the Environment, 20,* 71–93.

Deloitte (2011). *The millennial survey.* Retrieved March 28, 2013, from http:// www.deloitte.com/view/en_GX/global/about/business-society/7db3b035c9 3d4310VgnVCM2000001b56f00aRCRD.htm#. UVnOFzdc3vg

DHL (2011). *Corporate responsibility report.* Retrieved March 22, 2013, from http://www.dhl.com/content/dam/downloads/g0/about_us/DPDHL_CR% 20Report_2011.pdf

* DuPont. (2010). 2015 Sustainability Goals—DuPont Footprint. DuPont. The miracles of science. Retrieved January 2, 2010, from http://www2.dupont .com/Sustainability/en_US/Footprint/index.html

* Eccles, R. G., Ioannou, I., & Serafeim, G. (2011). *The impact of a corporate culture of sustainability on corporate behavior and performance, Harvard working paper.* Retrieved March 22, 2013, from http://hbswk.hbs.edu/item/6865.html

Ehrenfeld, J. (2008). *Sustainability by Design.* New Haven: Yale University Press.

* FedEx Global Citizen Report (2010). Retrieved July 25, 2012, from http:// about. van.fedex.com/sites/default/files/gcr/2010_FedEx_GCR.pdf

* Figge, F., & Hahn, T. (2004). Sustainable value added—measuring corporate contributions to sustainability beyond eco-efficiency. *Ecological Economics, 48*(2), 173–187.

Franca, C. L. (2013). Introductory approach to business model design for strategic sustainable development. Doctoral dissertation series No. 2013:08, Blekinge Institute of Technology, Department of Strategic Sustainable Development, Karlskrona, Sweden.

* Franca, C. L., Broman, G., Robért, K-H. Basile, G. Trygg, L. (2017). An approach to business model innovation and design for strategic sustainable development. *Journal of Cleaner Production,* 140. 155–166.

Frosch, R. A., & Gallopoulos, N. E. (1989). Strategies for manufacturing. *Scientific American, 261,* 144–152.

Gallop (2009). *The relationship between engagement at work and organizational outcomes.* Retrieved January 20, 2012, from www.gallop.com /consulting/126806/Q-12-Meta-Analysis.aspx.

* Global 100 (2012). *The global 100 most sustainable corporations in the world.* Retrieved July 11, 2012, from http://www.global100.org/annual-lists /2012-global-100-list.html

* Global Reporting Initiative (2013a). *G3.1 Guidelines.* Retrieved March 22, 2013, from https://www.globalreporting.org/reporting/latest-guidelines /g3-1-guidelines/Pages/default.aspx

Global Reporting Initiative (2013b). *G.3.1 Online.* Retrieved March 22, 2013, from https://www.globalreporting.org/reporting/guidelines-online/G31On-line/Pages/default.aspx

* Goldratt, E. (1984). *The Goal.* Great Barrington, MA: North River Press.

* Green Research (2012a). *The impact of Apple's withdraw from EPEAT,* July 10, 2012. Retrieved Mach 28, 2013 from http://greenresearch.com/2012/07/10/the-impact-of-apples-withdrawal-from-epeat/?utm_source=July+2012+Newsletter& utm_medium=email&utm_campaign=July+Newsletter

Green Research (2012b). *The annual sustainability executive survey, green research.* Retrieved from http://shop.greenresearch.com/products/annual-sustaianbility-executive-survey-2012. Cited by Hunter Lovins, *Employee engagement is key to sustainability success, sustainable brands website.* Retrieved March 28, 2013, from http://www.sustainablebrands.com/news_and_views/jul2012 /employee-engagement-key-sustainable-success

Grzybowska, K. (2012). Sustainability in the supply chain: Analysis of enablers, Chapter 2 within Golinska, P., & Romano C. A., (eds.), *Environmental Issues in Supply Chain Management, EcoProduction.* Berlin Heidelberg: Springer-Verlag. doi: 10.1007/978-3-642-23562-7_2.

* Handfield, R., Walton S. V., Sroufe, R. P., & Melnyk, S. A. (2002). Applying environmental criteria to supplier assessment: A study in the application of the Analytical Hierarchy Process. *European Journal of Operational Research, 141,* 70–87.

Hawkins, P., Lovins, A., & Lovins, H. (2008). *Natural Capitalism.* Little, Boston, New York and London: Brown and Company..

Hawks, K. (2006). VP Supply chain practice, Navesink. *Reverse Logistics Magazine Winter/Spring*. Retrieved March 28, 2013, from http://www.rlmagazine .com/edition01p12.php

Henretig, J. (2012). *Up in the Air*, Director of environmental sustainability, Microsoft, March. Article posted to *Sustainable industries*. Retrieved March 22, 2013, from http://www.sustainableindustries.com/articles/2012/03/air

* Hill, T. (2000). *Manufacturing Strategy: Text and Cases*. New York, NY: McGraw-Hill/Irwin.

Huang, Y. A., Weber, C. L., & Mathews, H. S. (2009). Categorization of scope three emissions for streamlined enterprise carbon footprinting. *Environmental Science Technology*, *43*(22), 8509–8515.

* Ignatius, A. (2012). Unilever CEO Paul Polman: Captain Planet. *Harvard Business Review*, 112–118.

* International Institute for Sustainable Development (2013). Retrieved March 22, 2013, from http://www.iisd.org/sd/

International Living Future Institute; https://living-future.org/

* Jana, R. (2008). Innovation: The biggest bang for the buck. *Indata*, September 22, 48.

Jensen, A. A., & Remmen, A. (2006). *Background report for a UNEP guide to life cycle management—a bridge to sustainable products*. Retrieved April 12, 2011, from http://lcinitiative.unep.fr/includes/file.asp?site=lcinit&file=86E47576 -EC54-4440-99B6-D6829EAF3622

* King, B. (2012a). Extended producer responsibility could help save $11 billion in recyclable Material, *Sustainable Brands Weekly*.

King, B. (2012b). *McDonalds recognizes sustainable supply chain partners from Sustainable Business Weekly*. Retrieved March 19, 2012, from http://www .sustainablebrands.com/news_and_views/articles/mcdonald%E2%80%99s -recognizes-sustainable-supply-chain-partners

* Kohli C., & Leuthesser L. (2001). *Brand equity: Capitalizing on intellectual capital*. Retrieved December 20, 2012, from http://www.iveybusinessjour- nal.com/topics/the-organization/brand-equity-capitalizing-on-intellectual- capital#. UNOCbqzNmSo

* Kollmus, A., Zink, H., & Polycarp, C. (2008). *Making sense of the voluntary carbon market: A comparison of carbon offset standards*. Stockholm Environ- mental Institute, World Wildlife Fund. Retrieved March 28, 2013, from http://www.globalcarbonproject.org/global/pdf/WWF_2008_A%20com- parison%20of%20C%20offset%20Standards.pdf

KPMG (2011a). *The corporate sustainability progress report*. Retrieved March 22, 2013, from http://www.kpmg.com/global/en/issuesandinsights/articlespub- lications/pages/corporate-sustainability.aspx

KPMG (2011b). *Sustainability reporting-what you should know.* Retrieved March 28, 2013, from http://www.kpmg.com/US/en/IssuesAndInsights/ ArticlesPublications/Documents/iarcs-sustainability-reporting-what-you-should-know. pdf

* Lambert, D., & Pohlen, T. (2001). Supply chain metrics. *International Journal of Logistics Management, 12*(1), 1–19.

* Lawrence Livermore National Laboratory (2012). *Estimated U.S. energy use for 2011, based on report department of energy.* Energy Information Association- 0384.

Lovins, H., & Cohen, B. (2011). *The Way Out: Kick-Starting Capitalism to Save Our Economic Ass.* New York, NY: Hill & Wang.

* Lovins, A. B., Lovins, L. H., & Hawkins, P. (2007). A roadmap for natural capitalism. *Harvard Business Review, 85,* 172–183.

Lubber, M. (2010). Compensation and sustainability. *Harvard Business Review, 21,* April 2010.

Lubin, D., & Esty, D. (2010). The sustainability imperative. *Harvard Business Review,* 43–5.

* Magretta, J., & Stone, N. (2002). *What management Is: How it Works and Why it's Everyone's Business.* New York, NY: Free Press.

Mathews, H. S., Hendrickson, C., & Weber, C. L. (2008). The importance of carbon footprint estimation bounds. *Environmental Science Technology, 42*(16), 5839–5842.

McDonald Corporation, (2012). *Global best of green 2012: Building a better business through effective practices around the World.* Retrieved November 25, 2012, from http://s3.amazonaws.com/mcdbestof-section-pdfs/1/MCD_076_BOG_ FINAL-ART_04.pdf

McDonough, W., & Partners (1992). *The Hannover principles design for sustainability.* Retrieved March 28, 2013, from http://www.mcdonough.com/principles.pdf

McDonough, W., & Braungart, M. (2002). *Cradle to Cradle.* New York, NY: North Point Press.

* McKinsey and Co., (2011). *Global survey results. The business of sustainability,* October, Sustainability and Resource Productivity Practice. Retrieved from http://www .mckinsey.com/business-functions/sustainability-and-resource-productivity /our-insights/the-business-of-sustainability-mckinsey-global-survey-results

McKinsey and Co. (2012). *From supply chains to supply circles.* Retrieved June 15, 2012 from http://www.mckinsey.com/Features/circular_economy

Meadows, D. H. (2008). *Thinking in Systems: A Primer.* White River Junction, VT: Chelsea Green Publishing.

* Melnyk, S. A. (1999). *Measurements, Metrics and the Value-Driven Operations Management System.* Atlanta, GA: Lionheart Publications.

Melnyk, S. A., Cooper, M. B., Griffis, S. E., Macdonald, J. R., & Phillips, C. L. M. (2010a). Supplier base management: A new competitive edge. *Supply Chain Management Review, 14*(4), 35–41.

Melnyk, S. A., Cooper, M. B., Griffis, S. E., Macdonald, J. R., Phillips, C. L. M. (2010b). Supplier base management: A new competitive edge. *Supply Chain Management Review, 14*(4), 35-41.

* Missimer M. (2015). Social sustainability within the framework for strategic sustainable development. Doctoral dissertation series No. 2015:09, Blekinge Institute of Technology, Department of Strategic Sustainable Development, Karlskrona, Sweden.

* MIT Sloan Management Review & Boston Consulting Group. (2013). *The innovation bottom line: Findings from the 2012 sustainability and innovation global executive study and research report.*

MIT Sloan Management Review and Boston Consulting Group (2012). *Sustainability nears a tipping point: Findings from the 2011 sustainability and innovation global executive study and research report.* Retrieved March 22, 2013, from http://c4168694.r94.cf2.rackcdn.com/MIT-SMR-BCG-Sustainability-Nears- a-Tipping-Point-Winter-2012.pdf

* Mohin, T. (2011). *How sustainability is driving employee engagement and the bottom line*, Greenbiz.com, September 29.

* Molloy, C. (2010). Cutting the carbon: Carbon disclosure project aims to foster a green economy. *Accountancy Ireland, 42*(6), 44–45.

Moore, G. (1991). *Crossing the Chasm*. New York, NY: Harper Business.

Nattrass, B., & Altomare, M. (1999). *The Natural Step for Business: Wealth, Ecology and the Evolutionary Corporation*. Gabriola Island, BC: New Society Publishers.

Natural Capitalism Solutions (2012). *Sustainability pays: Studies that prove the business case for sustainability.* Retrieved March 22, 2013, from http://www.natcapsolutions.org/

Nirenburg, I., & Sroufe, R. P. (2012). Model for sustainability. *Inside Supply Management, 23*(1), 30–31.

* OECD (2013). *OECD due diligence guidance for responsible supply chains of minerals from conflict-affected and high-risk areas.* Oecd.org. Retrieved February 8, 2013 from "OECD Due Diligence Guidance for Responsible Supply Chains of Minerals from Conflict-Affected and High-Risk Areas"

PE International (2010). *PE International handbook for life cycle assessment using the Gabi education software package*, PE International. Retrieved March 28, 2013 from http://www.gabi-software.com/fileadmin/gabi/tutorials/Paper- clip_Tutorial_Handbook_4.4.pdf

Polonsky, M., Rosenberger, P., & Ottman, A. (1998). Stakeholder's contribution to the green new product development process. *Journal of Marketing Management, 14*, 533–557.

* Porter, M. E., & Kramer, M. R. (2011). Creating shared value. *Harvard Business Review*, January–February.

* Procurement Intelligence Unit (2011). *By procurement intelligence staff.* Retrieved March 22, 2013, from http://www.procurementleaders.com/news-archive/news-archive/failure-to-mitigate-supply-chain-risk-to-cost-companies-billions-in-2012

* Puma (2011). *Puma completes first environmental profit and loss account which values impacts at € 145M*. Retrieved March 22, 2013 from http://about .puma.com/puma-completes-first-environmental-profit-and-loss-account-which-values-impacts-at-e-145-million/

Raelin, J. (2006). Does action learning promote collaborative leadership? *Academy of Management Learning and Education, 5*(2), 152–168.

Ravi, V., & Shankar, R. (2005). Analysis of interactions among the barriers of reverse logistics. *Tech Forecast & Social Change, 72*(8), 1011–1029.

Read, R. (2007). Dr. Russel Read, written testimony prepared for the U.S. senate banking subcommittee on securities, insurance and investment. In H. Lovins & B. Cohen (Eds.), *The Way Out: Kick-Starting Capitalism to Save our Economic Ass* (pp. 42). New York, NY: Hill and Wang Publishing.

* Saaty, T. L. (1990). How to make a decision—the analytic hierarchy process. *European Journal of Operational Research, 48*, 9–26.

Schein, E. (1993). *Organizational Culture and Leadership*. Fort Worth, TX: Harcourt College Publishers.

Scientific Applications International Corporation (SAIC) (2006). *Life cycle assessment: Principles and practice*. Retrieved May 13, 2011, from http://www.epa .gov/nrmrl/lcaccess/pdfs/600r06060.pdf

Senge, P., Lichtenstein, B., Kaeufer, K., Bradbufy, H., & Carroll, J. (2007). Collaborating for systemic change. *Sloan Management Review, 48*(2), 44–53.

* Shrivastava, P. (2007). Green supply chain management: A state-of-the-art literature review. *International Journal of Management Reviews, 9*(1), 53–80.

Spekman, R. E., & Hill, R. P. (1980). Strategy for effective procurement in the 1980s. *Journal of Purchasing and Materials Management*, 2–7.

Sroufe, R. P. (2003). Effects of environmental management systems on environmental management practices and operations. *Production and Operations Management, 12*(3), 416–432.

* Sroufe, R.P. (2016). Operationalizing sustainability. *Journal of Sustainable .Studies,* Issue 1.1

Sroufe, R. P., Curkovic, S., Montabon, F. L., & Melnyk, S. A. (2000). The new product design process and design for the environment: Crossing the chasm. *International Journal of Operations and Production Management, 20*(2), 267–291.

* Starbucks (2013). *Responsibly grown coffee*. Retrieved March 22, 2013, from http:// www.starbucks.com/responsibility/sourcing/coffee

Stika, N. (2010). *Sustainability drives recruitment and retention*, www.cosemin-spring.com; Mindspring.com, topics, sustainability, greening, June 9 2010.

* Supply Chain Operations Reference (2013). *Supply chain operations reference model overview-version 10*. Retrieved January 17, 2013, from http://www.supply-chain.org/

* Sustainable Land Development Initiative (SLDI) Code™ (2013). Retrieved April 2, 2013, from http://www.sldi.org/

* The Natural Step: http://www.naturalstep.org/

* Tiller, (2009). *Green survey*. Retrieved March 22, 2013, from http://www.tillerllc.com/pdf/TillerGreenSurvey2009.pdf

Touw, P. (2012). Chairman and CEO, ICIX, presentation 9/27/2012, *The new metrics of sustainable business, sustainable brands conference, presentation remarks* from "The Future of Technology Networks in Sustainability".

* Underwriters Laboratory and GreenBiz Group (2011). *UL 880: Standard for sustainability, manufacturing organizations* (1st ed.). Retrieved July 11, 2012, from http://www.ul.com/global/eng/pages/offerings/businesses/environment/services/sq/enterprisestandards/UL880/

* United Nations Global Compact and Business for Social Responsibility (2010). *Supply chain sustainability: A practical guide for continuous improvement*. Retrieved July 12, 2013, from http://supply-chain.unglobalcompact.org/site/article/68

United Nation's Sustainable Development Goals; https://sustainabledevelopment.un.org/sdgs

* UPS (2010). *Sustainability at UPS report*. Retrieved July 25, 2012, from http://www.responsibility.ups.com/community/Static%20Files/sustainability/UPS_AllPages.pdf

* U.S. Securities and Exchange Commission (2013). *Implementing Dodd-Frank Wall Street reform and consumer protection act—Pending Action*, Retrieved March 22, 2013, from http://www.sec.gov/spotlight/dodd-frank/dfactivity-upcoming.shtml#11-12-11

Walmart Supplier Sustainability Assessment (2013). *15 questions for suppliers*. Retrieved June 1, 2013, from http://az204679.vo.msecnd.net/media/documents/r_3863.pdf

* Willard, B. (2012). *The New Sustainability Advantage*, 10th Anniversary Edition. Canada: New Society Publishers.

* Womack, J. P., Jones, D. T., & Roos, D. (1990). *The Machine that Changed the World*. New York, NY: Free Press.

* World Business Council for Sustainable Development (2013). *Guide to corporate ecosystem valuation*. Retrieved March 22, 2013, from http://www.wbcsd.org/pages/edocument/edocumentdetails.aspx?id=104&nosearchcontextkey=true

Index

OTHER TITLES IN OUR ENVIRONMENTAL AND SOCIAL SUSTAINABILITY FOR BUSINESS ADVANTAGE COLLECTION

Robert Sroufe, Duquesne University

- *Strategy Making in Nonprofit Organizations: A Model and Case Studies* by Jyoti Bachani and Mary Vradelis
- *Developing Sustainable Supply Chains to Drive Value: Management Issues, Insights, Concepts, and Tools* by Robert Sroufe and Steven Melnyk
- *IT Sustainability for Business Advantage* by Brian Moore
- *A Primer on Sustainability: In the Business Environment* by Ronald M. Whitfield and Jeanne McNett
- *The Thinking Executive's Guide to Sustainability* by Kerul Kassel
- *Change Management for Sustainability* by Huong Ha
- *The Role of Legal Compliance in Sustainable Supply Chains, Operations, and Marketing* by John Wood
- *Feasibility Analysis for Sustainable Technologies: An Engineering-Economic Perspective* by Scott R. Herriott
- *ISO 50001 Energy Management Systems: What Managers Need to Know About Energy and Business Administration* by Johannes Kals

Announcing the Business Expert Press Digital Library

Concise e-books business students need for classroom and research

This book can also be purchased in an e-book collection by your library as

- a one-time purchase,
- that is owned forever,
- allows for simultaneous readers,
- has no restrictions on printing, and
- can be downloaded as PDFs from within the library community.

Our digital library collections are a great solution to beat the rising cost of textbooks. E-books can be loaded into their course management systems or onto students' e-book readers.
The **Business Expert Press** digital libraries are very affordable, with no obligation to buy in future years. For more information, please visit **www.businessexpertpress.com/librarians**.
To set up a trial in the United States, please email **sales@businessexpertpress.com**.